EDUCATION

AS A SOCIAL PROBLEM

EDUCATION
AS A SOCIAL PROBLEM

Six Lectures

by

RUDOLF STEINER

Dornach, August 9–17, 1919

ANTHROPOSOPHIC PRESS, INC.

NEW YORK

Translated from shorthand reports un-
revised by the lecturer, from the German edition published with the title,
Die Erziehungsfrage als soziale Frage
(Vol. 296 in the *Bibliographical Survey,*
1961). Translated by Lisa D. Monges
and Doris M. Bugbey.

This translation has been authorized for
the Western Hemisphere by the Rudolf
Steiner Nachlassverwaltung, Dornach,
Switzerland.

Printed in the United States of America

232891

FOREWORD

"A DEMAND for spiritual insight is sweeping like a great wave around the earth," said Rudolf Steiner in 1919. "The World War has made it necessary to seek a solution of the social question on the basis of spiritual fact, in accordance with reality."

At that time Germany was in chaos, people struggling just to keep body and soul together, trust in their leaders of the old order gone, the country on the verge of revolution. It was the moment for Rudolf Steiner to bring forward his idea of the "Threefold Social Order" for which he had been laying the groundwork through decades past in his researches into the true nature of Man. From January to April he had lectured in various cities about man's own threefold nature now pressing for expression in the outer forms of social life. Working people especially were eager to hear him, but he also spoke to prominent industrialists and to government officials, meanwhile writing articles for several magazines so as to reach a wider public. In April his book, *The Threefold Social Order,* was published.

During the summer he stressed the connections between social demands and the rejuvenation of educational methods

v

needed to meet those demands. Chief among these changes was, deepened knowledge of the spiritual forces at work in human life, and with it new concepts involved in the training of teachers. All this met with such enthusiastic response, particularly in the vicinity of Stuttgart, Germany, that plans were made at once for organizing a school to put the new methods into practice. It opened in that city in September with 126 children and a dozen teachers under Steiner's direct supervision, the first of the so-called Waldorf Schools which have since become known around the world.

In the midst of such intense activity, and striking into the very core of current social problems, Rudolf Steiner gave the series of six lectures printed herewith. It was given to members of the Anthroposophical Society, that is, to persons already familiar with his penetrating spiritual researches carried on during the previous twenty years. This series constituted another vital chapter in a year of the most vigorous efforts to sow seeds of enlightenment in a resistant, dark soil; seeds sown with hope, however, that they would one day sprout, grow, and bear fruit.

But first there were to be more world catastrophes before people were ready to wake up and commit themselves to radical, social change: economic collapse, the Great Depression, and a further prolonged spasm of World War. Afterward, again, a time of seeming recovery. Then, in the mid-sixties, began the spread of rebellion by those who were born at about the end of the second World War. They were of a new and very different generation, for they broke down all barriers and demanded new methods in education that would promote "human values" and new concepts for living.

Fifty years earlier Rudolf Steiner had seen these spiritual forces pressing to break through. Only now in 1968-9 have they thrown out their unquenchable challenge: Put an end to patchwork remedies and begin doing "what gets to the heart of things." It is highly important, therefore, to publish an English translation of these six lectures which do get to the heart of things in no uncertain terms.

Rudolf Steiner is not gentle here; not this time. He says we *must* slip free of the hold that materialistic reasoning has upon us, and give ourselves to *imaginative perception* of what is actually at work now in the world around us. Thus, when the reader encounters one startling statement after another, let him not be tempted to throw the book down and quit. Instead, if he is really serious in a desire to understand our ills, and seek remedies, let him take in the sharp, alien-sounding words—if such there be—until the total new picture takes shape and begins to work deeply into his sense of truth.

"Life" as we have assumed it to be—"The American Way" as we have known it—is here being dug up by the roots to let us see what cut-worms have been doing to it unbeknownst to us. It may take courage and determination to read the book to the end. But if one remains unbiased, and foregoes protest, arguing, and frustration along the way, the very effort made may well bring unimagined results for one's insight and creative action.

—*Doris M. Bugbey*

CONTENTS

ix

EDUCATION

AS A SOCIAL PROBLEM

I

A RECENT series of lectures and discussions with work-
men and co-workers in Stuttgart has given me deep insight
into what takes place in human souls at the present time, into
what exists as inner tragedy in mankind's evolution. Now I
am again able to spend a few days here in this place which
is so closely bound up with the work we must believe will
produce the force to guide the present tragedy of humanity
into more hopeful channels.

At no time perhaps has there been less inclination than
now to raise the soul to the spiritual worlds in true fashion,
and it is especially necessary now to do so.* Only from
these spiritual worlds can come the strength modern humanity requires if it is to go forward in its full humanness.
Today there is the most widespread belief that the problems
and tasks of the present can be resolved by the thoughts
and impulses derived from knowledge based on the external
world. How long it will take until a sufficiently large part

---

* See Rudolf Steiner's *Knowledge of the Higher Worlds and Its Attainment*
for what he means by "spiritual worlds."

of humanity will be convinced that real salvation is only attainable on the spiritual path, is extremely difficult to say, for the very reason that reflecting on this question is not fruitful. It is certain, however, that progress can only be made if sufficiently large numbers of people are permeated by the conviction that salvation can come only from the spiritual worlds.

What occupies people's minds today, in the widest circles, are the social problems. However, they lack the intellectual strength to earnestly study these problems, because in the present age the intellectual power of a great part of mankind is as though paralyzed. The belief prevails that the social problems can be mastered by what is called knowledge, but they can never be mastered if they are not tackled from the viewpoint of spiritual knowledge.

We have just passed through a long war. This will be followed by prolonged, perhaps very prolonged fighting by mankind in general. Many people have said that this war, which has been experienced throughout the civilized world, was the most terrible experience of its kind since the beginning of history. We cannot say that this judgment is wrong. The battle which will have to be fought by this or that means and which will follow this war—the battle between Orient and Occident, between Asia, Europe and America—will be the greatest spiritual battle ever waged by mankind. Everything that has flowed through the Christian world into humanity as impulses and forces will pour over civilization in tremendous, elemental waves of warfare.

It is possible to state today in a simple formula the great contrast between the Orient and Occident. But this simple formula—do not take it as simple. It contains an enormous quantity of human impulses. You know that in my book *The Threefold Social Order* I drew attention to the fact that for extensive circles of present-day humanity spiritual life has become an "ideology"; that what constitutes men's spiritual properties—rights, customs, science, art, religion, and so on—is looked upon as merely a vapor rising from the only true reality, from the economic means of production, the economic foundation. I spoke to you about these matters when I took leave of you here several months ago.

"Ideology." That is the answer many people give today when spiritual life is spoken of. It is all something that is mirrored in the human soul from the only reality, the economic reality; it is mere "ideology." There is much reason to reflect on the real meaning of this word "ideology" in world culture for it means a great deal. One can connect this word with no other word more closely than with the word "maya" of oriental wisdom. "Maya"—"illusion"—properly translated into occidental language means "ideology." Every other translation of this word is less exact. Thus we may say: The same concept that the Oriental connects with the word *maya* is connected by a great part of western humanity with the word *ideology*. But what a tremendous difference! What does the Oriental think when he uses the word *maya?* He thinks that the external world is *maya;* everything that confronts our senses and the intellect bound up with them is *maya,* the great illusion, and the only reality is what arises in the soul. What a human being achieves in the sphere of soul and spirit, that constitutes reality. What arises and pours forth from man's

5

inner life is reality. What presents itself externally to the senses is maya, illusion, ideology.

The opposite conviction, that the only reality is what presents itself to the outer senses, is spread over a great part of Western humanity. Precisely what the Oriental calls *maya* constitutes reality for a great part of Western mankind; and what the Oriental calls reality, that which blossoms and wells up in the soul, constitutes *ideology*, illusion, for a large segment of Europe and America.

You see here a great contrast. This makes deep inroads into men's souls; it shapes them across the earth into two quite distinct kinds of beings. If you survey what has happened in the civilized world in recent years you will say —I hope: Fundamentally speaking, everything that is said about the reasons for this world catastrophe is just skimming the surface, is merely superficial opinion. What has expressed itself in this terrible fighting has arisen with elemental power from unconscious depths. It can be clearly seen today that people participated in this fighting without knowing the reason for it. It is the expression of what this contrast, which will not be resolved for a long time, has brought to the surface as elemental forces. The anti-social element at present is so strong that it has split mankind into these two essentially different parts.

If you connect what I have just stated with other things I have explained to you, you will find that the striving of the West is for *freedom*. No matter whether this freedom is understood or misunderstood, the longing for freedom wells up as if from dark foundations of the human soul. Turn your gaze to the East. What is called freedom in the

West has no real meaning for the East; no concepts or feelings are connected with it. *We do not think about what we experience most intensely.* Just consider how little attention people give to the phenomena of nature surrounding them every day. They do not think about their immediate experiences. The Oriental, in pursuing the reality natural to him, the inner reality, lives in the freedom he derives from the peculiarities of his race, his folk, and his tribe. He does not think about it. The further we look toward the West the more we become aware of the fact that freedom has been lost in the course of the historical evolution of mankind. Because the Western peoples do not have it they have to strive for it.

We could cite many more instances; in every one of them we would find this fundamental difference between West and East. There is already a first indication of what perhaps will occur in the next few years. At the moment this manifests in outer symptoms taking place in Asia and about which Europe is still silent today—silent for well-known reasons. The fact, for instance, that more than half the population of India is near starvation will bring to birth, out of the spirituality of the Indian nation, something that will be very different from what has happened in Europe. These are outer symptoms. But also in regard to these outer symptoms mankind is divided today into two essentially different parts. For the Indian hunger signifies something totally different from what it means to the European, because the Indian has behind him a soul development throughout millennia which is quite different from that of the European. These facts have to be sharply focussed by anyone who wants to comprehend the course of mankind's evolution. Today we must be clear that what is usually called the social question is something much more complicated than is ordinarily imagined. This social question is an accompanying phenomenon of the culture that arose after the middle of the fifteenth century. I have repeatedly spoken to you about this significant incision in the history of civilized mankind in the midde of the fifteenth century. Since that time natural science has gradually arisen in its modern coloring. During that period, however, industrialism also has arisen in its modern coloring. Natural science and industrialism have been poured over modern humanity and have given it its particular spiritual trend.

I have spoken to you about the special nature of this natural science and have told you that intelligent people, who today reflect on what natural science has to offer, say: What it offers is not the world, it is rather a specter of the world. Everything scientists have thought out and that has become popular education, all this—much more so than is ordinarily imagined—is belief in a spectral world; actually superstition. And along with this world of specters there exists the spiritual effect modern industrialism has had upon men.

We must give attention now to the spiritual significance of this industrialism. Consider what primarily controls it—the machine. A machine is different from everything else man makes use of in outer life. Just consider the animal. If you turn your scientific or other thoughts to an animal—I will not speak today of man in this connection—you can carry on any amount of research concerning an animal but something always remains, something of a deep and divine essence. You cannot fathom an animal; you cannot discover its secrets. There is always something behind your thoughts about an animal that remains unknown. This is no less the case with a plant. Take even a crystal, the wonderful forms of the crystal world. You will have to say: Certainly we can grasp the external nature of the crystal world, its forms and so on, if we are trained in this respect, but much remains that man can revere and to which his ordinary, non-clairvoyant intellect does not penetrate.

Now consider a machine. It is entirely transparent to our thinking. We know how its power is produced, know the position of its pistons, the magnitude of friction. We can calculate its efficiency if we know the various factors; there is nothing behind the machine which would lead us to say that it cannot be penetrated by the ordinary, non-clairvoyant intellect. This is of great significance for the mutuality of man and machine. And when one has stood once again before many thousands of people who have to do with machines, one knows what it is that drips into these souls from the spiritually transparent machine. For the machine has nothing behind it that can only be divined, something not surveyable by man's non-clairvoyant intellect. That fact that a machine is soul-spiritually so completely transparent that its power and power-relationships lie clearly open before the human senses and intellect—this fact makes contact with machines so disastrous for mankind. That is what sucks out the human heart and soul, making man dry and inhuman.

9

Natural science together with the machine threatens civilized humanity with a terrible threefold destruction. Now what is this danger threatening modern man if he does not make up his mind to look to the supersensible? In regard to knowledge, that ideal presses to gain control which the scientists describe as follows: One endeavors to arrive at an astronomical way of thinking about nature; that is, thinking fashioned after the pattern of astronomy. When the modern chemist thinks about the content of a molecule he thinks of the atoms within the molecule as being in a certain force relationship. He conceives of it in the form of a small planetary and solar system. To explain the whole world astronomically becomes an ideal. And astronomy itself, what is its ideal? To conceive of the whole world-structure as a machine! Now add to this the work people do by machine!

These are the influences that have become increasingly strong since the middle of the fifteenth century and rob men of their humanness. If they were to continue thinking in the way they think about machine-like astronomy and about the industrialism in which they work, human spirits would become mechanized; human souls vegetized, sleepy; and human bodies animalized.

Look toward America, the climax of the mechanization of the human spirit! Look toward the European East, toward Russia, the wild and frightful impulses and instincts that run riot there—the animalization of the body. In the middle, in Europe, the sleepiness of the soul. Mechanization of the spirit, vegetizing of the soul, animalization of the

body—this is what we have to face without deceiving ourselves.

It is characteristic of humanity's path since the middle
of the fifteenth century that not only two life-elements have
been lost but also a third. Today a powerful party puts forward "social democracy." In other words, it welds together
socialism and democracy although they are the opposite of
each other. This party welds them together and leaves out
the spirit. For socialism can only refer to economic life,
democracy only to the sphere of civil rights, and individualism would refer to spiritual life. Freedom has been
omitted from the phrase "social democracy," otherwise
it would have to be called "individualistic social democracy."
Then all three aspects of human concern would come to
expression in such a title. But it is characteristic of the
modern age that the third element has been omitted; that
the spirit has really become *maya,* the great illusion for
civilized humanity of the West, for Europe and its colonial
outgrowth, America. This is what we have to bear in mind
when we consider spiritual science in the sense of a great
cultural question. What lives in the demands of the present
cannot in reality be a subject for discussion. *These are
historical demands.* Socialism is an historical demand. But
liberalism, freedom, individualism, these also are an historical demand, although they have been little noticed by
modern men. People will no longer have anything to say
unless they establish the social organism in the sense of the
threefold order: socialism for economic life, democracy for
the life of rights, and individualism for spiritual life.

This will have to be looked upon as the real, the only salvation of mankind. But we must not delude ourselves about the fact that precisely these intensive, unyielding historical demands of the present age create other demands for one who has deeper insight into these matters. Adults will have to live in a social organism which, in regard to the economic aspect, will be social; in regard to government, democratic; and from the spiritual aspect, liberal, free. The great problem of the future will be that of education. How will we have to deal with children so that they, as adults, can grow into the social, democratic, and spiritually free areas of living in the most comprehensive way? Spiritual science has pointed to this problem of education as present-day humanity will have to understand it if it wishes to advance. Social demands will remain chaotic if it is not seen that at their base lies the most urgent problem of the present time: the problem of education. If you wish to acquaint yourselves with the broad guide-lines concerning this problem of education you only need to study my little book, *Education Of The Child From The Point Of View Of Spiritual Science*. Here one of the most important questions of the present time has been brought to the surface, namely, the social question of education. The widest circles of modern humanity will have to learn what spiritual science has to offer in regard to the three epochs of man's youth and their development.

In this book it has been pointed out that between birth and the seventh year, which is the year when the change of teeth occurs, a child is an imitative being, he does what he sees in his surroundings. If you observe him with real understanding you will find that he is an imitative being who does what the grownups do. It is of utmost importance for a child that the people in his surroundings do only what he may imitate; indeed, that they think and feel only what is wholesome for him to imitate. When a child enters physical existence he only continues the experiences he had in the spiritual world prior to conception. There we live, as human beings, within the beings of the higher hierarchies; we do what originates as impulses from the nature of the higher hierarchies. There we are imitators to a much higher degree because we are united with the beings we imitate. Then we are placed into the physical world. In it we continue our habit of being one with our surroundings. This habit then extends to being one with, imitating, the people around us who have to take care of a child's education by doing, thinking, and feeling only what he may imitate. Benefit for a child is all the greater the more he is able to live not in his own soul but in those within his environment.

In the past when man's life was more instinctive he could also rely instinctively on this imitation. This will not be the case in future. Then care will have to be taken that a child be an imitator. In education the question will have to be answered: How can we best shape the life of a child so that he may imitate his surroundings in the best possible way? What has happened in the past in regard to this imitation will have to become increasingly intensive and conscious in the future. For men will have to make clear to themselves that when children are grown to adulthood in the social organism they will have to be free human beings, and *one can become free only if as a child one has been a most intensive imitator.* This natural power of a child must be strongly developed precisely for the time when socialism will break in upon us. People will not become free beings, in spite of all declaiming and political wailing about freedom, if the power of imitation is not implanted in them in the age of childhood. Only if this is done will they as adults have the basis for social freedom.

From the seventh year of life until puberty, until the fourteenth and fifteenth year, there lives in a child what may be called action based on authority. When a child undertakes what he does because a revered personality in his surroundings says to him, "This is right, this should be done," then it is the greatest blessing that could happen to him. Nothing is worse than for a child to get accustomed to making his so-called own judgments too early, prior to puberty. A feeling for authority between the ages of seven and fourteen will in future have to be developed more intensively than has been done in the past. All education in this period of life will have to be consciously directed toward awaking in a child a pure, beautiful feeling for authority; for what is to be implanted in him during these years is to form the foundation for what the adult is to experience in the social organism as the equal rights of men. Equal rights among men will not come into existence in any other way, because *people will never become ripe for these equal rights if in childhood regard for authority has not been implanted in them.* In the past a lesser degree of feeling for authority might have sufficed; in future it will not be so. This feeling will have to be strongly implanted

14

in a child in order to let him mature for that which is not open to argument but arises as an historical demand.

All primary school education in our time must be organized in a way to let people attain this view of the situation. Now I ask you: How far are people today, how far is modern teacher-training from an insight into these things? How must we work if this insight is to be gained? *And it must be gained,* because only if this is firmly achieved can salvation come.

If today one visits those countries which have the first revolution already behind them, what does one experience in regard to their programs for so-called "consolidated schools"? What are their programs? To the person who has insight into the relationships existing in human nature, their socialistic educational programs are the most terrifying imaginable. The most awful, frightening things to be thought out and placed before mankind today are the school programs, the curricula, the organized education connected with the name *Lunatscharski,* the Russian Minister of Education. The educational program developed in Russia murders all true socialism. But also in other regions of Europe the educational programs are actually cancerous evils, particularly the socialist programs of education, because they proceed from the almost unbelievable principle that schools must be established after the pattern of adult life in the social organism. I have read school programs whose first principle is the abolition of head-masters; the teachers should stand in a relationship of absolute equality with the students, the entire school should be built up on comradeship. If one speaks against such a principle today, let us say in South Germany where matters have not advanced as far as other regions in this respect, then one is branded as a person who does not understand anything about social life.

Those people, however, who are in earnest in regard to the creation of a truly social organism, must above everything else be clear about the fact that such an organism can never arise with the socialistic programs for education. Because, if socialism is introduced into schools it cannot exist in life. People become mature for a socially just life together only if during their school years their life has been built upon true authority. We must realize today how far removed from any sense of reality is what people do and think.

After puberty, between the fourteenth and twenty-first years, not only the life of sexual love develops in man; this develops merely as a special manifestation of universal human love. This power of universal human love should be specially fostered when children leave the primary school and go to trade schools or other institutions. For the configuration of economic life, which is a demand of history, will never be warmed through as it should be by brotherly love—that is, universal human love—if this is not developed during the years between fourteen and twenty-one.

Brotherliness, fraternity, in economic life as it has to be striven for in future, *can only arise in human souls if education after the fifteenth year works consciously toward universal human love.* That is, if all concepts regarding the world and education itself are based on human love, love toward the outer world.

Upon this threefold educational basis must be erected what is to flourish for mankind's future. If we do not know that the physical body must become an imitator in the right way we shall merely implant animal instincts in this body. If we are not aware that between the seventh and fourteenth year the ether body passes through a special development that must be based on authority, there will develop in man merely a universal, cultural drowsiness, and the force needed for the rights organism will not be present. If from the fifteenth year onward we do not infuse all education in a sensible way with the power of love that is bound to the astral body, men will never be able to develop their astral bodies into independent beings. These things intertwine. Therefore, I must say:

> Proper imitation develops freedom;
> Authority develops the rights life;
> Brotherliness, love, develops the economic life.

But turned about it is also true. When love is not developed in the right way, freedom is lacking; and when imitation is not developed in the right way, animal instincts grow rampant.

Thus, in dealing with this problem you see that spiritual science is the proper basis for what must become the content of culture precisely because of the great historical demands that arise today for mankind. Without this content of culture, which can flow only from spiritual science, we cannot make any progress. That is to say, the questions confronting us must be brought into a spiritual atmosphere; this, as a conviction, must enter human souls. I should like to emphasize once more that the length of time it will take for such a conviction to take root may be debated, but in any case what people unconsciously strive for can in no way be reached unless this conviction lays hold of them. I believe you can see from this the connection between what has been carried on in various fields through our spiritual science and what arises from the distress of the age as the great historical necessities for mankind in the present and immediate future. This was the reason for my statement that spiritual science must be considered in its relationship to the great historical tasks of the present. Of course, people are far, far from judging matters in the way I have characterized. There must first arise in them a tension of dissatisfaction, so that out of the very opposite, purely materialistic striving there may arise the striving for spirituality. Otherwise, how are people to tackle the problem that has led them to use the expressions *maya,* and *ideology,* so adversely?

What has resulted from this? You will realize that the impulses behind Oriental and Occidental thinking are very different; but the peculiar thing is that they have produced the same feeling throughout both. This soul orientation has to be considered. That the people of the East described the outer world as *maya* is of ancient origin. This mystical concept of the world had its great significance then, but it is not significant at present. Because in a sense it has become outmoded the Orient has been overtaken by a certain passive surrender to it; by a false fatalism which, through the Turkish element, has influenced Europe in the crudest manner. Fatalism, an attitude of let-happen-what-may, signifies the passivity of the human will.

In the most precise way the Occidental concept of *ideology* arose in the same sphere of fatalism through Marx and Engels. This concept is the modern socialistic doctrine that everything of a soul-spirit nature originates in the one and only reality, the economic process, and so is *maya, ideology.*

How did this doctrine arise? By bringing something fatalistic into the world. Up to the catastrophe of the World War what then was the outer expression of the socialistic doctrine? It was: Capital accumulates, concentrates; bigger and bigger groups of capitalists arise, trusts, monopolies, etc. The economic process of increased concentration of capitalistic groups will run its course quite by itself until the moment arrives when, of itself, the control of capital passes to the proletariat. Nothing has to be done to bring it about, it is an objective, purely economic process. Fatalism.

The Orient arrived at fatalism: the Occident proceeds from fatalism, the majority of the people supporting it. Most of the people are fatalistic. To submit to what the world process is to bring has become the principle of the Orient. It is also the principle of the Occident. For the Orient, however, it is submission to something spiritual; for the Occident it is submission to the material, economic process. In both cases human evolution is seen in a one-sided way. But if we survey evolution as it is today, resulting from former conditions, we find in it a spiritual element that has become *ideology,* as I have described. This spiritual element is based on Greek culture. The deepest impulse of our souls has a Greek character. Therefore, we have the classical school (*Gymnasium*), which is an imitation of the Greek soul structure in education. In Greece this soul structure was natural to the growing child up to puberty, for the great mass of the people were the poor people, the slaves, the helots, who were excluded from such education. The conquerors were of different blood. They were the bearers of spiritual life, justifiably so. You can see this expressed in Greek sculpture. Look at a Mercury head (I have often mentioned this) with the special position of the ears, nose, and eyes. In this head the Greeks pointed to that part of the population they had conquered and to whose care they left the outer life of trade, the economy. The spirit had been bestowed by cosmic powers upon the Aryan, characterized by the head of Zeus, of Hera, of Athene.

Do not believe that the Greek soul structure comes only to expression in the general soul constitution. It also expresses itself in the formation of word and sentence in the Greek language. This rests upon an aristocratic soul structure. We have this still in our spiritual life. When the middle of the fifteenth century approached, we did not experience a renewal of spiritual life but only a Renaissance or a Reformation, a refurbishing of the old.

We educate our youth in the classical schools estranged from life. It was self-evident for the Greeks to educate their youth as we do in our *Gymnasium,* because that was their life. They educated their children and their youth in accordance with their life; we educate youth in our classical schools according to Greek life. For that reason our spiritual life has become world-estranged and is considered to be *ideology*. Its thoughts are too short-sighted to take hold of life, and, above everything else, to intervene actively in life through deeds.

Beside this element of spiritual education there lives in us a strange education in the field of law. It can be shown in all spheres of life that the middle of the fifteenth century constitutes a mighty incision in humanity's evolution. Grain is expensive today, and everything produced from grain is expensive. It is excessively expensive! If one investigates when it was excessively cheap in European countries one comes to the ninth and tenth centuries. At that time it was just as much too cheap as today it is too expensive. But in the middle of the fifteenth century it had a normal price.

It is interesting to see how, right down to the price of grain, the fifteenth century shows this great incision in history. At that time when the price of grain was fair over a great part of Europe, the ancient serfdom gradually ceased to exist. But then, in order to destroy this beginning of freedom, Roman law started to become dominant. Today, in the sphere of politics, of rights, we are permeated by Roman law, just as we are permeated in the sphere of spiritual life by the spirit and soul structure of the Greeks. In the sphere of rights we have been unable to produce anything but a renaissance of Roman law. So in our social organism we have the Greek spiritual structure and the Roman State structure.

Economic life cannot be shaped as a renaissance. Of course, it is possible to live according to Roman law, and we can educate our children according to the spiritual structure of the Greeks; but we cannot eat what the Greeks ate because this would not satisfy our hunger. Economic life must arise as a part of the present time. Thus we have the European life of economics as the third element. Since these three areas of living are chaotically intermingled, it is necessary that we bring order into them. This can only be done through the threefold social organism.

In a most one-sided manner people like Marx and Engels have realized that, for they recognized that it will no longer do to govern with a spiritual life that originates in ancient Greece; nor will it do to live with a government that has been derived from Roman law. Nothing remains but economic life, they said, so they concentrated exclusively upon that. Engels said: In future only commodities and the processes of production must be administered and directed; human beings must no longer be governed. This is just as one-sided as it is correct; correct, but terribly one-sided.

Economic life must rest on its own basis. Within the economic member of the social organism only goods—commodities—must be managed and the processes of production directed. This must become independent. But if one eliminates from the social organism the life of rights and the spiritual life in their old form, one must establish them in a new form. That is to say, alongside economic life, which manages goods and directs the processes of production, we need the democratic life of the state, which is based on the equality of men. We need not a mere renaissance of Roman law but a new birth of the life of the state on the basis of the equality of men. We need no mere renaissance of spiritual life as it existed at the beginning of the modern era. We need a new form, a new creation of spiritual life. We must become conscious of the fact that we are really confronted now with the task of creating spiritual life anew.

What has been stated by the demand for the threefold order of the social organism is connected with that which in the deepest sense lives in the development of modern humanity. This idea is not the result of a brainstorm, it is something born of the deepest needs of our age, something that corresponds in the highest degree to our present time. There are many people who say they do not understand this, that it is very difficult. In Germany, when people said over and over that these things are difficult to understand, I said to them that I certainly do make a distinction between these ideas and what one has become accustomed to understand during the last four or five years. There one thought it easy to understand things I could not understand—so I said—things that merely had to be commanded to be understood. The Supreme Headquarters or another place of authority commanded that matters had to be understood, then they certainly were crammed into one's head. They were understood because one was commanded to understand. What is of importance now is to understand something out of one's free human soul. To that end it is necessary for people to wake up. For this, however, there is very little inclination, yet events will depend upon it. Difficulties do not arise from a subject being incomprehensible, but from a lack of will. It is courage that is lacking, courage to look into this reality. It is self-evident that what must speak in a new tone to humanity must be formulated in sentences different from those which men have been accustomed to thus far. For we have been taken hold of by three things that are different from what this threefold order of the social organism requires.

In this threefold order a renewal of spiritual life is demanded in a way that lets people feel a vital connection of their soul with objective spiritual life. They do not now have this connection. When people speak today they speak in hollow phrases. They do this because they have no relationship to what these hollow phrases are supposed to express. Men have lost their connection with the life of the spirit, therefore their words have become empty talk.

Much has been said about rights in recent years, about the establishment of rights among civilized mankind. The events of the present time demonstrate sufficiently how far removed from reality men are today in regard to human rights. They have not fought for rights, only for power, but they have talked about rights.

Now how is it with economic life? There have been no thoughts that would have encompassed economic life, therefore events have taken place of themselves. The characteristic factor in economic life has been continuous production, as I described it in Vienna in the spring of 1914 when I called this continuous producing of goods a social cancer. Commodities were produced and thrown on the market at random; the whole economic process was to take

24

place of itself, not thoughtfully directed. A chaotic economic life without direction; a life of rights become a mere striving for power; a spiritual life degraded to hollow phrases: this is the threefold character of social life we have had and of which we must rid ourselves. We can only get rid of it if we know how to take seriously what is meant by the threefold order of the social organism.

But this can only be understood if we relate it back to anthroposophically oriented spiritual science. People were annoyed when in a public lecture some weeks ago I made a statement which, however, is a fundamental truth. I said: The leading circles of the present time must no longer rely on their brain, which has become decadent. They must rise to a comprehension that does not need the brain, but the ether body. For the thoughts that must be laid hold of in our spiritual science do not need the brain. The leading circles, the middle class of today, the bourgeoisie, just because of their physiological development, must submit to the development of spiritual knowledge that can be fostered even with decadent brains.

The proletariat, the working class, strives upward. It still has unused brains. The lemon hasn't yet been completely squeezed dry; something of an atavistic character still comes out of the brain. Therefore, the proletariat still understands what is said in the sense of the new order of things. The situation today is such that the entire proletariat would be receptive to these things, but not their leaders, for they have become bourgeois. They have become greater philistines than the real philistines. They have taken over philistinism and have developed it into a high culture. But on the other hand there exists a terrible penchant for obedience. This obedience will first have to be broken, otherwise there will be no salvation here either.

You see, matters are more complicated in the present age than we ordinarily imagine, and only the science of initiation can lead to a real taking hold of the social problems of our time. There are three concepts you may also find in my book, *The Threefold Social Order*, which I have written not only for anthroposophists but for the general public. You will find three important concepts in present-day social life: (1) the concept of commodity, the product, the goods in economic life; (2) the concept of labor; (3) the concept of capital. The social thinking of the present adheres to these three concepts.

How much has been proclaimed in social science in order to comprehend these three concepts! Whoever knows what has arisen in the second half of the nineteenth century on the subject of a scientific national economy, trying to penetrate these concepts of commodity, labor, and capital, knows the impossible science the economists have achieved. It is totally inadequate. I have recently quoted a neat example of this. The famous Professor Lujo Brentano, the luminary of national economic science in middle Europe at the present time, has recently written an article entitled, *The Entrepreneur,* in which he develops three marks of distinction for the enterpriser. I shall only mention the third one, the use of the means of production at one's own risk. The enterpriser is the owner of the means of production and un-

26

dertakes production for the market at his own risk. Now, Brentano so formulates his concept in that article that he is able to designate a further enterpriser beside the manufacturer and industrialist, namely, the modern laborer. The workman is an enterpriser because he has the means of production, that is, his own labor-force, and this he offers on the market at his own risk. Mr. Brentano's concept of the enterpriser is crystal clear as it includes the laborer among the enterprisers. This shows how clever modern economic science is! It is ridiculous. But people are not willing to ridicule such matters because the universities still take the leading positions in spiritual life. Yet this is what universities produce in the field of national economy. People do not have the courage to confess that what is produced in this field is ridiculous. Matters are really dreadful.

Our attention, however, must be focussed upon such things, therefore we must ask: Why is it that precisely in regard to social concepts, which at present become burning questions of the day, all science is inadequate? It would give me great satisfaction if I could speak to you more in detail about this question during my present stay here. Today I shall only give a short report.

Although the concept "commodity" is merely economic it can never be formulated with ordinary science. You will not arrive at the concept of "commodity" if you do not base it upon imaginative knowledge. You cannot grasp "labor" in the social, economic life if you do not base it upon inspired knowledge. And you cannot define "capital" if you do not base it upon intuitive knowledge.

The concept of commodity demands imagination;

The concept of labor demands inspiration;

The concept of capital demands intuition.*

If you do not form these concepts in this manner only confusion results.

You can see in detail why such confusion must result. Why does Brentano define the concept of "capital," which coincides with the concept "enterpriser," in a way to designate the laborer a capitalist? Because he is a very clever man of the present day but has no idea that, in order to gain a real concept of capital, intuitive knowledge is needed!

In a certain roundabout way the Bible points to this when it speaks of capitalism as "mammonism." It connects capital with a certain kind of spirituality, but spirituality can only be recognized by intuition. If we wish to recognize the spirituality active in capitalism—mammonism—we need intuition. We find this already in the Bible. But today we need a world conception that raises this to the modern level.

These matters, which today may still be considered queer, must be penetrated by expert knowledge. Real, expert knowledge in this sphere will result in the demand for a penetration of social concepts by genuine, true, spiritual science. This forces itself today upon the unbiased observer of life. If you were present, you will remember the memorable question that was asked at the end of my lecture at the Bernoullianum in Basel, delivered before my journey. In the following discussion a man asked: "How can it be brought about that Lenin become the ruler of the world?"

* See *Knowledge of the Higher Worlds and Its Attainment.*

For, in that man's opinion there is no hope unless Lenin rules the world.

Just consider the confusion! Those men who today behave most radically are the most reactionary. They want socialism. Above everything else one ought to begin by socializing rulership, but they start their socialism with the universal economic monarchy of Lenin! Not even a beginning is made to socialize the relationships of rulership. This is how grotesque things are today. The real situation should be kept in mind if someone says to you that Lenin ought to become world ruler. Those who believe they have the most enlightened concepts have the most perverted ones, and clarity in this sphere cannot be attained if there is no will to seek this clarity in the science of the spirit.

II

Dornach, August 10, 1919

IF WE WISH to understand the task of the anthroposophical science of the spirit in the present and immediate future we must consider the character of mankind's evolution since the middle of the fifteenth century. Everything that happens now depends on the fact that since that time there lives in mankind the impulse for each single individuality to attain the pinnacle of personality, to become a whole personality. This was not possible, nor was it the task of mankind in earlier epochs of our post-Atlantean evolution. If we want to understand this great change in the middle of which we find ourselves, we must focus our attention still more precisely upon such matters as I characterized yesterday.

I said that in our spiritual life we still have a Greek constitution of soul. The way we form our thoughts, the manner in which we are accustomed to think about the world, is an echo of the Greek soul. And the way we are accustomed to look at civic rights and everything connected with them is an echo of the soul-constitution of the Roman. In the State we still see the structure as it existed in the Roman

Empire. Only if people will realize that the impulse of the threefold social order must enter our chaotic present will there be clarity in thinking and willing.

The soul-nature of the Greek was chiefly determined by the fact that in Greece there existed in the highest degree what were the leading characteristics of historical development right up to the middle of the fifteenth century. Across the Greek territory there were spread a subject population and their conquerors. These latter claimed the land for themselves; but also, through their blood inheritance, they determined the spirituality of ancient Greece. We cannot grasp the soul-nature of the ancient Greeks unless we keep in mind that it was considered justified to think about human relationships in the way that resulted from the blood characteristics of the Aryan conqueror population. Naturally, modern man has outgrown what thus lay at the basis of Greek culture. With the Greeks it was self-evident that there were two kinds of people: those who had to worship Mercury, and those who had to worship Zeus. These two classes were strictly separated. But, people thought about the world and the Gods in the way the conqueror population had to think because of its blood characteristics. Everything resulted from the clash of a conquered and conquering people. One who looks more closely into what lives socially among men of our time will recognize that in our feelings and our subconscious soul-life we no longer have this aristocratic attitude in viewing our world. Yet it still lives in our ideas and concepts, especially if we are educated in the schools of higher learning. These schools, especially the classical schools, shape their instruction in a way that represents a renaissance, and echo of Hellenism. And this is even more the case with our universities, with the exception of the technical and agricultural colleges which have sprung from modern life. Even they imitate in their outer form the structure of universities derived from Hellenism. Through the very fact that we have a high esteem for Hellenism in its time, and for its time, we must also be quite clear about the necessity for our age of a renewal of spiritual life. It will become more and more unbearable for humanity to be led by souls who have acquired the form of their concepts in our classical schools. And today, in almost all leading positions, you find people who did receive the forming of their ideas in the classical schools. It has become necessary today to realize that the time of "settling accounts," not minor but major accounts, is at hand, and that we must think about such matters factually and stop clinging to old habits of thought.

You know that what was formed out of the blood in Hellinism became abstract in Romanism. I have mentioned this here before. The Greek social organism, which cannot be called a State organism, shaped itself out of forces descending through the blood. But this did not pass over to Romanism. What did pass over was the urge to organize as the Greeks had organized, but the cause of this organizing was no longer felt to be in the blood. While it would never have occurred to an ancient Greek to doubt that there are people of a "lower sort," those in a conquered people, and others being of a "higher sort," the Aryans, this was not the case with the Romans. Within the Roman Empire there was the strong consciousness that the order of the social

32

organism had been arrived at through power, through might. You need only remind yourselves that the Romans trace their origin to that assembly of robbers in the neighborhood of Rome that had been called together in order, as a robber band, to found Rome; and that the founder of Rome was not suckled with delicate mother's milk but, as you know, was suckled in the forest by an animal, a wolf.

These are the influences that were taken up into the Roman nature and led to the formation of the social order in Rome largely out of abstract concepts. What has remained as our heritage in regard to the concepts of rights and the State has thus come from the Roman constitution of soul.

In this connection I am always reminded of an old friend of mine. I met him when he was already quite advanced in years. In his youth, at the age of eighteen, he had fallen in love with a girl and they had secretly become engaged. But they were too poor to marry, so they waited and remained faithful to each other. When he finally could consider marriage he was sixty-four years old, for only then had he acquired enough means to risk taking such a step. So he went to his home town near Salzburg ready to marry his chosen one of so long ago. But alas, the church and the rectory had burned down and he could not get his baptismal certificate. There was no record of his baptism anywhere, so there was no proof that he had been born. I remember vividly the day his letter arrived. It stated, "Well, I believe it is quite evident that I was born, for after all I exist. But these people do not believe I was born because there is no baptismal certificate to prove it."

I once had a conversation with a lawyer who said, "In a lawsuit it is not so important whether or not a man is present; all we need is his birth certificate."

Continually one meets such grotesque incidents. The mood living in them shows that our entire public life has been built to a greater or lesser degree on Romanism. We are citizens of the world not through the fact we have become and exist as human beings but because we are recorded and recognized in a certain office. These things all lead back to Romanism. The descent by blood has passed over into registration.

Today the situation is such that many men no longer consider their value determined by what they are as human beings but by the rank they have reached in the hierarchy of officialdom. One prefers to be something impersonal, out of Roman rights-concepts, rather than a personality. Since the fifteenth century, however, there exists in mankind the subconscious striving to base everything on the pinnacle of personality. This shows us that in regard to spiritual life and the life of rights the times have changed and we need a renewal of both, a real renewal. This is connected with many deeper impulses of mankind's evolution.

Just consider the fact that since the middle of the fifteenth century the evolution of modern man has been filled with the natural-scientific mode of thought which is based on abstract laws of nature, upon sense perception and the thoughts developed around it. Only what is derived from sense perception is considered valid. Yesterday I drew your attention to the fact that today there are quite a number of people who are convinced, justifiably so, that a view of

34

nature acquired in this way can only lead to a ghost-like image of nature. A picture of the world formed by a student of nature is a specter of the world, not the real world. So we have to say that humanity finds itself in the position of developing a specter-image of the world in regard to one half of it. For the science of initiation something profound is concealed behind this, and what this is we must now consider.

Sense perception as such cannot be altered; whether we consider it to be *maya* or something else is of no concern to a deeper world view. A red flower is a red flower whether or not we think it *maya* or *reality*. It is what it is. Likewise, all sense perception is what it is. Discussion starts only when we begin to form thoughts about it, when we consider it to be this or that, when we interpret it. Only then the difficulty begins. It begins because the concepts we as men have to form since the fifteenth century are different from those of earlier mankind. No attention is paid to this in modern history, which is a *fable convenue,* as I have often stated. Whoever is able to understand the concepts of mankind prior to the middle of the fifteenth century knows that they were full of imagery, that they actually were imaginations. The present abstraction of concepts exists only since that time.

Now why has our human nature so developed that we have these abstract concepts we are so proud of today and that we constantly employ? They have the peculiar character that, although we make use of them in the sense world they are not suited to this sense world. They are worthless there. In my book, *The Riddles of Philosophy,* I have expressed this by saying that the way man forms his concepts regarding the external world constitutes a side-stream of his soul development. Think of a seed in the earth; it is destined by nature to become a plant. But we take many seeds and grind them into flour and eat them as bread. This, however, is not what the seed is meant for; it is a lateral development. If we ask, doesn't the seed contain those chemical elements we need for building up our body? we must say that it does not lie in the nature of the grain of wheat or rye to nourish us but to bring forth new grain. Likewise, it does not lie in our nature to grasp the outer world through the concepts we have acquired since the fifteenth century. We shall reap something different from those concepts if we enter into their nature properly. These modern concepts are the shadow images of what we have experienced in the spiritual world before birth—more exactly, before conception. Our concepts, the forces in them, are the echos of what we have experienced before birth. We misuse our system of concepts in applying it to the outer sense world.

This is the basis of Goethe's concept of nature. He does not want to express the laws of nature by means of concepts; he strives for the primal phenomena. That is to say, he strives for the assembled outer perceptions, because he feels that our conceptual ability cannot be applied to external nature. We have to develop our conceptual ability *as pure thinking*. If we do so, it points us toward our spiritual existence prior to birth. Our modern thinking has been bestowed upon us so that we may reach with this pure thinking our spiritual nature as it existed before we were

36

clothed with a physical body. If mankind does not comprehend the fact that it possesses thinking in order to apprehend itself as spirit, it does not take hold of the task of the fifth post-Atlantean period. Our natural science was inserted, so to say, into mankind's destiny so that we might remain with pure nature and not speculate about it. We were to employ our concepts to perceive it in the right way, and then develop our concepts in order to behold ourselves as we existed in spirit before we descended into the physical body. Men still believe today that they should only employ their conceptual ability for classifying external sense perceptions, and so on. However, they will only act correctly if they employ the thoughts they have had since the middle of the fifteenth century for perceiving the spiritual world in which they existed before they acquired a physical body.

In this way man of the fifth post-Atlantean era is forced toward the spiritual, toward the existence before birth. And still another factor places him in a peculiar situation which he must develop. Parallel to the specter-concepts of natural science runs industrialism, as I mentioned yesterday. Its chief characteristic is the fact that the machine, the bearer of industrialism, is spiritually transparent. Nothing of it remains incomprehensible. As a consequence the human will directed toward the machine is, in truth, not directed toward a reality. In terms of comprehensive world-reality the machine is a chimera. Industrialism introduces something into our lives which in a higher sense makes man's will meaningless. There will be a significant impact on social life when modern men become convinced that the machine and everything resulting from it, such as industrialism, makes the human will meaningless. We have already reached the pinnacle of machine activity. Today a quarter of all production on earth is not being produced by human will but by machine power.* This signifies something extraordinary. Human will is no longer meaningful on earth.

If you read, for instance, the speeches of Rabindranath Tagore, you ought to sense something in them that remains incomprehensible to the European who employs his ordinary intellect. There is a different tone in what an educated Asiatic has to say today, because in him this adaptation of the European spirit to the machine is completely incomprehensible. To the Oriental the activity of working by means of machines, by means of industrialism, has no meaning. The European may believe it or not, but European politics born in the machine age is also just as senseless to the Oriental. In the educated Oriental's statements there is clearly expressed that this one-fourth of human labor in the present age is felt by him as senseless work—this quarter which is not carried out by the educated Orientals but only by Occidentals and their imitators, the Japanese. The Oriental feels so because, as he still possesses much clairvoyant vision, he knows that labor performed by machines has a definite peculiarity. When a man plows his field with his horse—man and beast straining themselves in labor—this work in which natural forces are involved has a meaning beyond the immediate present; it has cosmic meaning. When a man kindles fire by using a flint, making the sparks ignite the tinder, he is connected with nature. When the wasp builds its house this natural activity too has cosmic

* By 1969 this amount, of course, has been greatly increased.—Tr.

38

meaning. Through modern industrialism we have abandoned cosmic value. In our kindling of electric flames there no longer lives any cosmic significance. It has been driven out. A completely mechanized factory is a hole in the cosmos, it has no meaning for cosmic evolution. If you go into the woods and collect firewood this has cosmic meaning beyond earth evolution; but a modern factory and everything it contains has no significance beyond earth development. The human will is inserted in it without its having any cosmic value. Just consider what this means. It means that since the middle of the fifteenth century we have developed a knowledge that is specter-like and does not touch reality. More and more we employ machines and carry out an industrial activity, and the will inserted into this activity is senseless for world evolution.

The great question now confronts us: Is there nevertheless a meaning for mankind's evolution as a whole in the fact that our knowledge is ghost-like, and our will to a great extent senseless? Indeed there is meaning in it, significant meaning. Mankind thereby is to be urged to penetrate beyond ghost-like thinking to a knowledge of reality that does not stop with the perception of nature but enters into the spiritual behind nature. So long as men received the spirit simultaneously with their concepts they did not need to make efforts to gain the spirit. Since in the modern age men have only retained concepts devoid of spirit, but that also contain the possibility of working one's way up to the spirit as I have stated, there is present in man the impulse to proceed from abstract knowledge and to penetrate into genuine spiritual knowledge. Therefore, since we have industrialism with its senselessness we must seek another meaning for human will. This we can only do if we arouse ourselves to a world view that brings sense into what is senseless— let us call it industrialism—by deriving meaning from the spiritual, saying: We seek tasks that stem from the spirit. Formerly, when willing could derive its impulses from the spirit instinctively, we did not need to arouse ourselves especially in order to will from out the spirit. Today it is necessary that we make a special effort to do this. The senseless industrial willing has to be confronted with a meaningful willing-out-of-the-spirit.

Yesterday I gave you an example of the way we ought to educate. We should recognize that up to the seventh year man is an imitator since he develops chiefly his physical body during this period. Imitation, therefore, ought to become the basis for that period of education. We should know that from the seventh to the fourteenth year we have to develop man by the principle of authority. This spiritual knowledge, which we gain by knowing how the etheric body develops during that time, must be made the impulse of education then. We should know also how the astral body develops from the fourteenth to the twenty-first year, and that this knowledge must lie behind education for that period. Then, only then, do we will out of the spirit.

Up to the middle of the fifteenth century man willed instinctively out of the spirit. In external life we tend to immerse ourselves in machines, in mechanism; this is so even in politics, which gradually has turned governments into machines. We must strive for a spirit-ensouled willing. To that end we must accept the idea of a science of the spirit. We must, for instance, base education on what we know out of spiritual facts, out of what we learn from anthroposophical spiritual science. Through the stronger, more conscious emphasizing of willing out of the spirit we establish a counter-image to the senseless willing of industrialism.

Thus, industrialism with all its devastation of the human soul, is given us in order that in this devastation we may rouse ourselves to will out of the spirit. Our thinking has to be changed in many ways in our modern age. This requires a careful, intimately developed feeling for truth. We must become conscious that the feeling for truth has to be gradually applied in places where we are not yet accustomed to apply it. I believe many a person will be astonished today if he is told: You are right if you venerate Raphael highly because of his pictures, but if you demand that people paint the way Raphael painted then, you are mistaken. Only he has a right to admire Raphael who knows that whoever paints today the way he painted is a bad painter, because he does not paint as the impulses of our time demand. One does not feel with the times if one does not deeply sense the tasks of a given age. It is necessary that we acquire in our time an intimate feeling for truth in this regard. But here also modern humanity is caught up in what is the very opposite. One gets the impression that the feeling for truth has everywhere sprung a leak and does not function. People are shying away from calling right what is right, and wrong what is wrong; they recoil from designating a lie a lie. We experience today the most abominable things, and people are indifferent to them. The point is that we should have such a feeling for truth that we know, for example, that Raphael's painting no longer fits our present age; that it must be considered as something of the past, and admired as such. It is particularly necessary now to pay attention to such things when out of the depths of the soul the impulse for truth comes over us. I am often reminded of a beautiful passage in Herman Grimm's biography of Michelangelo in which he speaks of his Last Judgment. He says that many such Last Judgment pictures were painted at that time and that the people experienced in full reality the truth of what was painted on the walls. They lived in the truth of those pictures. Today we should not look at such a picture as Michelangelo's Last Judgment without being aware that we do not feel as those people did for whom the artist painted it; that we have lost their feeling and at best can say: This is the picture of something we no longer believe in as an immediate reality.

Just consider how differently man confronts such a picture with his modern consciousness. He no longer thinks that angels really descend, or that the devils carry on as they do in Michelangelo's picture. If, however, one is aware that what modern man feels when looking at this picture is something gray and abstract, then one is called upon inwardly to experience the whole living movement in these pictures on the wall of the Sistine Chapel. One is stirred to asking how it was possible for the people of Michelangelo's time (although he painted after the decline of the fourth post-Atlantean period his paintings originated in the spirit of that period since he stood at the boundary of the fourth and fifth periods)—how was it possible for people like him and his contemporaries to experience such tremendous imaginations, such mighty pictures? This question confronts us in all its magnitude if one is conscious of how drab and lifeless is what man feels today in front of such a picture by Michelangelo. We must ask: What caused human souls of that time to conceive of the earth's end in such a way? Whence came the structure of these pictures?

The reason lies in the following: Since the time when the Mystery of Golgotha entered earth evolution and had given it its meaning, certain things that existed in the ancient manner had to recede into the background and were destined to be regained by mankind later on. One of these was the idea of repeated earth lives. The totality of human life takes its course through earth life, then life in the spiritual world, then earth life again, and so on. This course of the total life of man was the content of the atavistic, instinctive world-view in ancient times. Christianity had to arouse in man concepts different from those of ancient wisdom. By what means, above all, has Christianity accomplished this? It directed human consciousness only to a certain point in time, namely, to the beginning of one's life on earth. It did not consider man as an individuality prior to birth or conception but merely as a thought of the Godhead. Before earth-life man proceeds out of the spiritual world as a thought of the Godhead, only at birth did he begin to be a real human being. Then, after his life on earth, the life after death. In the first period of the development of Christianity the experience of repeated earth lives was, so to say, misplaced. Human experience was limited to looking into the origin of man and the life after death. This, how-

43

ever, supplied the equilibrium out of which the pictures of the Last Judgment were created. *Through the fact that Christianity first eradicated from human feeling the teaching of pre-existence,* the pictures of the Last Judgment could arise. Today there wells up again out of the deep recesses of the human soul the longing for a recognition of repeated earth lives. Therefore, those pictures fade away which only focus their attention upon the one earth life and a vague spiritual world before and after it. Now there exists the most intense longing to enlarge the Christian world-view of the early ages. The Mystery of Golgotha is not merely effective for those who believe only in one earth life, it is also valid for those who know of repeated earth lives. The present age is in need of this enlargement. Therefore, we should see clearly that we live in a period when we must use the ghost-like nature of ordinary conceptual knowledge, and the senselessness of willing released by industrialism, in order to rise to spiritual knowledge and spirit-permeated willing, as I have described it; and also in order to enlarge religious consciousness so as to include repeated earth lives.

The great and full importance of this enlargement of human consciousness in the present time should be deeply inscribed in the soul of modern men, for upon this depends whether they really understand how to live in the present, and how to prepare the future in the right sense. Everyone, in the situation in which life has placed him, can make use of this enlarged consciousness. Even the external knowledge people gain will cause him to demand something that today plays a large role in the subconscious depths of soul life but that has difficulty in rising and sounding out into full consciousness. Truly, the most striking fact of modern life is that there are so many torn human souls; souls full of problems who do not know what to do with life, who ask again and again, "What precisely is my task? What does life mean to do specifically with me?" They start this or that and yet are never satisfied. The number of these problematic natures increases steadily. What is the reason for it? It comes from a lack in our educational system. Today we educate our children in a way which does not awaken in them the forces that make man strong for life. Man becomes strong through being an imitator up to his seventh year; through following a worthy authority up to the fourteenth year; and through the fact that his capacity for love is developed in the right way up to the twenty-first year. Later on this strength cannot be developed. What a person lacks because the forces were not awakened which should have been awakened in definite periods of his youth—this is what makes him a problem-filled nature. *This fact must be made known!*

For this reason I had to say yesterday that if we will to bring about a true form of society in future it must be prepared through people's education. To this end we must not proceed in a small way but on a large scale; for our educational system has gradually taken on a character that leads directly to what I described yesterday as mechanization of the spirit, vegetizing of the soul, and animalization of the body.

We must not follow this direction. We must strongly develop the forces that *can* be developed in a child's soul, so that later on he can harvest the fruits of his childhood learning. Today he looks back and feels what his childhood was, and cannot gather anything from it because nothing was developed there. Our educational principles must be fundamentally changed if we want to do the right thing for children. Above everything we must listen very carefully to much that at present is highly praised and considered especially wholesome.

So, it is necessary that, without undue strain and exertion but through an economy of educational effort, children acquire concentration. This can be achieved, in the way modern man needs it, only by abolishing what is so greatly favored today, namely, the cursed curriculum of the schools; this instrument of murder for the real development of human forces. Just consider what it means: From 7 to 8 A.M. arithmetic, from 8 to 9 grammar, from 9 to 10 geography, from 10 to 11 history. Everything that has moved through the soul from 7 to 8 is extinguished from 8 to 9, and so on. Now here it is necessary to get down to the bottom of things. We must no longer think that subjects exist in order to be taught *as subjects*. On the contrary, we must have clearly in mind that in children from the seventh to fourteenth year, *thinking, feeling,* and *willing* have to be developed in the right way. Geography, arithmetic, everything must be employed so that these faculties can be properly developed.

Much is said in modern pedagogy about the need of developing individualities, of paying attention to a child's nature in order to know which faculties should be developed. This is empty talk. These questions take on meaning only when they are discussed from the point of view of

46

spiritual science, otherwise they are mere phrases. In the future it will be necessary to say that for a certain age group we must impart a certain amount of arithmetic. Two or three months are to be devoted to teaching arithmetic in the forenoon. Not a plan of study that contains everything jumbled up but arithmetic for an extended time, then on to another subject. Arrange things as they are indicated by human nature itself for definite points in time.

You see the tasks that arise for a pedagogy which works toward the future. Here lie the positive problems for those who seriously think about the social future. As yet there is little understanding for these problems. In Stuttgart, connected with our previous activities, a school is to be built up as far as possible within the present school system. Mr. Molt has decided to found such a school for the children of his employees in the Waldorf-Astoria Cigarette Factory.* Other children will be able to come, but at first of course only in limited numbers. Naturally, we will have to take into account the educational goals of the State. The children will have to achieve this and that by the end of a year, and we will have to make certain compromises. But we will be able to intermix something with what the State requires, because, according to socialistic ideas, the State is the specially clever idol. So we shall have to intermix with what it demands that which is required by the real nature of man. This has to be recognized. But who today thinks of the fact that the prevailing plan of study is the murderer of truly

* In the course of the next ten years this "Waldorf School" became the largest private school in Germany, with a waiting list of applicants from several European countries and the United States.

47

human education? There are people whose thoughts in this direction are such that one is inclined to say: The world stands on its head, one has to turn it back on its legs. For many would shorten the lessons and change the subjects every half hour. This today is considered ideal. Just imagine: Religion, arithmetic, geography, drawing, singing, one after the other. In our heads they tumble through each other like the stones of a kaleidoscope. Only the outer world says, "Now that's something like it!"—because there is not the slightest interrelating between these subjects.

Few believe it is necessary now to think on a large scale; not to think petty thoughts but to have great, comprehensive views. We experience again and again that people finally have become accustomed to saying, "Indeed, revolution is necessary!" Even a large part of the bougeoisie believes today in revolution. I do not know if that is the case here, but there are large areas where a majority of the bourgeoisie believes revolution to be necessary. But if we offer them such things as are stated in my book, *The Threefold Social Order,* they say: "We do not understand this. It is too complicated." Lichtenberg once said, "If a head and a book strike together and a hollow sound results it is not necessarily the fault of the book." But people do not believe this, because—it is not self-knowledge that is chiefly produced in men's souls. One can experience that throughout extensive regions the philistines believe in revolution, yet they say, "O no, we cannot enter into such deep questions, such comprehensive thoughts; you must tell us how shoe production can be socialized, how the pharmacies are

48

to be socialized," and so on. "You must tell us how, in the revolutionized State, I can sell my spices."

One gradually discovers then what these people really mean. They mean that they agree there must be a revolution, but everything should remain as it has been, nothing should be changed by it. Many a person asks, how can we make the world over?—but so that nothing is changed! The most remarkable ones in this respect are the so-called intellectuals. With them one can have the most extraordinary experiences. One heard it repeatedly stated, "Very well, three members—autonomous universities, a spiritual life that governs itself—but then, how shall we live? Who will pay our salaries if the State no longer pays us?"

Today we really have to confront these things. It is necessary that we stop turning away from these questions again and again. Precisely in the sphere of the spiritual life a change must be brought about.

III

Dornach, August 11, 1919

WHAT I have to say today will be a kind of interlude. I should like to speak briefly about three concepts which, if they are fully understood, can bring about an understanding of outer social life. I say expressly *outer* social life because these three concepts originate from people's cooperation in outer affairs. I refer to the concepts commodity, labor, capital. I have already told you that modern political economy in all its shadings endeavors in vain to arrive at complete clarity about these concepts. That was not possible after men began to think consciously in a political-economic fashion. Prior to the middle of the fifteenth century there can be no question of people consciously comprehending their mutual social relationships. Life took its course more or less unconsciously, instinctively, in regard to the social forces playing between man and man. Since then, however, in the age when the consciousness-soul is being developed, people have had to think more and more consciously about social relationships. And so, every kind of idea and direction in the life of human society has arisen. This begins with the school of the

Mercantilists, then the school of the Physiocrats, Adam Smith, the various Utopian streams, Proudhon, Fourrier, and so on, right up to modern social-democracy on one side and modern academic political economy on the other.

It is interesting to compare the modern social-democratic theory based on Marx and Engels, with modern academic political economy, which is completely unproductive. It produces no concepts capable of permeating the social will. Nothing results from the confused, chaotic concepts of modern academic political economy if we pose the question of what is to happen in social life, because this academic economy is infected by the concepts of modern science. You know that in spite of the great and admirable progress of natural science, which is not denied by spiritual science, this modern science in the schools and universities completely rejects all that springs from the spirit. As a result political economy wants only to observe what happens in economic life. But this has become almost impossible in recent times because the more people have evolved in the modern age the less have they had thoughts that could cope with economic facts. Economic facts took their own course mechanically, as if by themselves; they were not accompanied by human thinking. Therefore, observing these thought-bereft facts of the world market cannot lead to laws, and has not done so, because our political economy is practice without theory, without ideas, and our social-democratic endeavors are theory without practice. The socialistic theory can never be put into practice, for it is a theory without insight into practical life. We suffer in modern times from the fact that we have an economic life that is practice without ideas, and with it the mere theory of the social democrats without the possibility of introducing this theory into economic life. Thus we have reached a turning point in the historical evolution of mankind.

Since social life has to be founded upon the relation of man to man it will be easy for you to realize that a certain attitude has to underlie all human endeavor to found a socially just life. That is what is so important in the threefold membering of the social organism, namely, that this certain attitude, this feeling, be generated in the interrelated spheres of social action. Without this mood of soul among men social life cannot flourish. This soul quality will definitely be taken into account by the threefold social organism. I should therefore like to point today to certain aspects of this matter.

If you think of social life as an organism you will have to imagine that something of a soul-spiritual nature streams through it. Just as in the human and animal organism the blood is the bearer of the air that is inhaled and exhaled, so something must breathe through, must circulate through the entire social organism.

Here we come to a chapter that is hard for modern man to comprehend because he is so little prepared for it; but it must be comprehended if there is to be any question at all of a social reformation. The fact that in the social life of the future the content of human conversation will be of special significance, is something that must be understood. Results will depend upon what people take seriously when they exchange their ideas, their sensations, their feelings. The views that hold sway among men are not insignificant if they wish to become social beings. It is necessary for the future that general education be governed not merely by concepts derived from science or industry, but by concepts that can be the basis for imaginations. Improbable as it may seem to modern man, nevertheless it will not be possible to develop a social life if people are not given imaginative concepts; that is to say, concepts which shape the human mind quite differently from the merely abstract concepts of cause and effect, energy and matter, and so forth, that are derived from natural science. These concepts derived from science which govern everything today, even art, will be of no avail in the social life of the future. For that we must make it possible again to comprehend the world in pictures.

What is meant by that I have repeatedly indicated, also in regard to the question of education. I have said: If we intimately occupy ourselves with children it is easy to impart to them, let us say, the idea of immortality by showing them the chrysalis of a butterfly, how it opens and the butterfly emerges and flies away. We then can make clear to the child, "Your body is like the chrysalis, and in it there lives something like the butterfly, but it is invisible. When you come to die, with you too the butterfly emerges and flies into the spiritual world." Through such comparisons we bring about an imaginative effect. But we must not merely think out such a comparison; this would only be acting in the manner of the scientific view. What is the attitude of people with present-day education as they hear such a comparison? Modern men, even when they are barely grown up, are very clever, exceedingly clever. They do not consider at all that one might be clever differently from the way they, in their abstract concepts, deem themselves clever. Men are very peculiar in regard to their modern cleverness!

A few weeks ago I gave a lecture in a certain city. It was followed by a meeting of a political science association in which a university professor—a clever man of our time, of course—spoke about my lecture and what was connected with it. He was of the opinion that not only the views I had advanced but also those to be found in my books, are infantile. Well, I understand such a judgment. I understand it especially well when the man is a university professor. I understand it for the reason that science, which he represents, has quite lost all imaginative life and considers infantile what it does not comprehend. It is characteristic of modern men in their cleverness that they say: If we are to employ such an image, which compares the immortal soul with the butterfly emerging from the chrysalis, we, the clever ones, know that it is an image we have made; we have passed beyond the content of such an image. But the child is childlike, so we compare what we know in our concepts with this image, yet we ourselves do not believe in it. The secret of the matter is, however, that in that case the child does not believe in it either. The child is only taken hold of by the picture if we ourselves believe in it. The genuine spiritual-scientific attitude is to restore in us the faculty of seeing in nature not the ghost-like things of which science speaks, but the pictorial, the imaginative. What emerges from the chrysalis and is present in the butterfly is really an image for the immortality of the soul placed into the order of nature by the divine world order. If there were no im-

54

mortal soul there would be no butterfly emerging from the chrysalis. There can be no real image if truth is not the basis for it. So it is with all of nature. What natural science offers is a ghost. We can comprehend nature only if we know that it is an image for something else.

Likewise, people must accustom themselves to considering the human head as an image of a heavenly body. The human head is not round in order to resemble a head of cabbage, but rather to resemble the form of a celestial body. The whole of nature is pictorial and we must find our way into this imagery. Then there will radiate into the hearts, the souls and minds, even into the heads—and this is most difficult—what can permeate man if he takes in pictures. In the social organism we will have to speak with each other about things that are expressed in pictures. And people will have to believe in these pictures. Then there will come from scientific circles persons able to speak about the real place of commodities in life, because the commodity produced corresponds to a human need. No abstract concepts can grasp this human need in its social value. Only that person can know something about it whose soul has been permeated by the discernment that springs from imaginative thinking. Otherwise there will be no socialization. You may employ in the social organism those who rightly ascertain what is needed, but if at the same time imaginative thinking is not incorporated in the social organism through education it is impossible to arrive at an organic social structure. That means, we must speak in images. However strange it may sound to the socialistic thinker of today, it is necessary that in order to arrive at a true socializing we must speak from man to man in pictures, which induce imaginations. This indeed is how it must happen. What is a commodity will be feelingly understood by a science that gains understanding through pictures, and by no other science.

In the society of the future a proper understanding of labor will have to be a dominating element. What men say today about labor is sheer nonsense, for human labor is not primarily concerned with the production of goods. Karl Marx calls commodities crystallized labor power. This is nonsense, nothing else; because what takes place when a man works is that he uses himself up in a certain sense. You can bring about this self-consumption in one way or another. If you happen to have enough money in the bank or in your purse you can exert yourself in sports and use your working power in this way. You also might chop wood, or do some other chore. The work may be the same whether you chop wood or engage in a sport. The important thing is not how much work-power you exert, but for what purpose you use it in social life. Labor as such has nothing to do with social life insofar as this social life is to produce goods or commodities. In the threefold social organism, therefore, an incitement to labor will be needed which is completely different from the one that produces goods. Goods will be produced by labor because labor has to be used for something. *But that which must be the basis for a man's work is the joy and love for work itself*. We shall only achieve a social structure for society if we find the methods for inducing men to want to work, so that it becomes natural for them, a matter of course, that they work.

This can only happen in a society in which one speaks of inspired concepts. In future, men will never be warmed through by joy and love for work—as was the case in the past when things were instinctive and atavistic—if society is not permeated by such ideas and feelings as enter the world through the inspiration of initiates. These ideas must carry people along in such a way that they know: We have the social organism before us and we must devote ourselves to it. That is to say, work itself takes hold of their souls because they have an understanding for the social organism. Only those people will have such understanding who have heard and taken in those inspired concepts; that is to say, those imparted by spiritual science. In order that a love for work be re-born throughout mankind we cannot use those hollow concepts proclaimed today. We need spiritualized sciences which can permeate hearts and souls; permeate them in such a way that men will have joy and love for work. Labor will be placed alongside commodities in a society that not only hears about pictures through the educators of society, but also hears of inspirations and such concepts as are necessary to provide the means of production in our complicated society, and the necessary foundation upon which men can exist.

For this we further need to circulate intuitive concepts in society. The concepts about capital that you find in my book, *The Threefold Social Order*, will only flourish in a society which is receptive to intuitive concepts. That means: Capital will find its rightful place when men will acknowledge that intuition must live in them; commodity will find its rightful place when the necessity for imagination is acknowledged; and labor will find its rightful place when the necessity of inspiration is acknowledged.

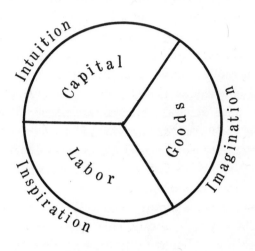

Figure 1.

If you take the above diagram and do not write the three concepts one below the other but in the way I have done here, then you can learn a lot from it if you permeate it with all the concepts to be found in my book about the threefold membering of the social organism. There are connections, back and forth, between labor and commodities; between commodities and capital, inasmuch as capital buys commodities; connections between labor and capital, and so on. Only, these three concepts must be arranged as shown.

Above everything, we must understand it is correct to say that in future the social order must become humanized. But it is necessary also to understand that the social order must be brought into being by men themselves; that they be willing to make up their minds to listen to the science of the initiates about imaginations, inspirations, and intuitions. This is a serious matter, for I am herewith stating nothing less than the fact that without the science of the spirit there will not take place in future any social transformation. That is the truth. It will never be possible to arouse in men the understanding necessary for matters like intuition, inspiration, imagination, if you abandon the schools to the State. For what does the State make out of schools?

Just think of something which has eminently to do with both the school and the State. I must confess I think it is something terrible, but people do not notice it. Think of civil rights, for example.* These rights are supposed to arise in the sense of those practices people today consider the proper thing. Parliaments decide about civil rights (I am speaking of democracy, not at all of monarchy). Civil rights are established through the representatives of everyone who has come of age. They are then incorporated in the body of law. Then the professor comes along and studies the law. Then he lectures on what he finds there as the declared civil rights. That is to say, the State at this point takes science in tow in the most decided way. The professor of civil rights may not lecture on anything but what is declared as rights in the State. Actually, the professor is not even needed, because one could record the State's laws

* Translators' note: It must be emphasized that in Rudolf Steiner's social thinking these rights are only those which apply to everyone equally. It rules out the special connotations the expression has acquired in recent years, particularly in the United States of America.

59

for a phonograph and place this on the speaker's desk and let it run. This then is science.

I am citing an extreme case. You will scarcely assert that the majority decisions of parliaments today are inspired. The situation will have to be reversed. In spiritual life, in the universities, civil rights must come into existence as a science purely out of man's spiritual comprehension. The State can only attain its proper function if this is given to it by people. Some believe that the threefold membering of the social organism wants to turn the world upside down. Oh, no! The world is already upside down; the threefold order wishes to put it rightside up. This is what is important.

We have to find our way into such concepts or we move toward mechanizing the spirit, falling asleep and vegetizing the soul, and animalizing the body.

It is very important that we permeate ourselves with the conviction that we have to think thus radically if there is to be hope for the future. Above everything it is necessary for people to realize that they will have to build the social organism upon its three healthy members. They will only learn the significance of imagination in connection with commodities if economic life is developed in its pure form, and men are dependent upon conducting it out of brotherliness. The significance of inspiration for labor, producing joy and love for work, will only be realized if one person joins another as equals in parliaments, if real equality governs; that is, if every individual be permitted to contribute whatever of value lives in him. This will be different with each person. Then the life of rights will be governed by equality and will have to be inspired, not decided upon by the narrow-minded philistines as has been more and more the trend in ordinary democracy.

Capital can only be properly employed in the social organism if intuition will rise to freedom, and freedom will blossom from out the independently developing life of the spirit. Then there will stream out of spiritual life into labor what has to stream into it. I shall indicate the streams by arrows (Figure 2). When so organized these three spheres will permeate one another in the right way.

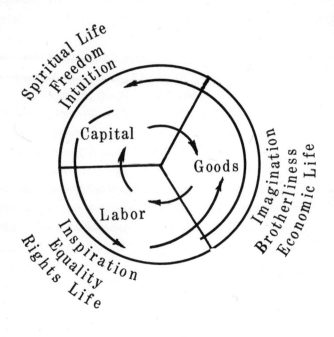

Figure 2.

One of the first objections I met with in Germany was that people said: "Now he even wants to 'three-member' the social organism! But the social organism must be a unity!" Men are simply hypnotized by this idea of unity, because they have always considered the State as something uniform. They are accustomed to this concept. A man who speaks of this unity appears to me like a man who says, "Now he even wants to have a horse that stands on four legs; a horse must be a unity, it cannot be membered into four legs." Nobody will demand such a thing, of course, nor do I wish to put the "horse" State, the social organism, on one leg but upon its healthy three legs. Just as the horse-unit does not lose its unity by standing on four legs, likewise the social organism does not lose its unity by placing it upon its healthy three members. On the contrary, it acquires its unity just by placing it upon its healthy three members. Men today are entirely unable to free themselves from their accustomed concepts. But it is most important that we do not merely believe that single external establishments have to be transformed, but that it is our ideas, our concepts, our feelings that have to be transformed. Indeed, we may say that we need different heads on our shoulders if we wish to approach the future in a beneficial way. This is what is necessary and what is so hard for men to get accustomed to, because our old heads are so dear to us, these old heads that are only accustomed to thinking what they have thought for ages. Today we have consciously to transform what lives in our souls.

Now do not think this is an easy task. Many people believe today that they have already transformed their thoughts; they do not notice that they have remained the same old ones, especially in the field of education. Here you can have strange experiences. We tell people of the concepts spiritual science produces in the field of education. You may talk today to very advanced teachers, directors, and superintendents of schools; they listen to you and say, "Well, I thought that a long time ago; indeed, I am of exactly the same opinion." In reality, however, they hold the very opposite opinion to what you tell them. They express the opposite opinion with the same words. In this way people pass each other by today. Words have lost connection with spirituality. It has to be found again or we cannot progress.

Social tasks, therefore, lie much more in the sphere of the soul than we ordinarily realize.

IV

Dornach, August 15, 1919

FROM the various matters we have considered here you will have gathered that among the many problems under discussion today that of education is the most important. We had to emphasize that the entire social question contains as its chief factor, education. From what I indicated a week ago about the transformation of education it will have become clear to you that within the whole complex of this subject the training of teachers is the most important auxiliary question. When we consider the character of the epoch that has run its course since the middle of the fifteenth century it becomes evident that during this period there passed through mankind's evolution a wave of materialistic trials. In the present time it is necessary that we work our way out of this materialistic wave and find again the path to the spirit. This path was known to humanity in ancient cultural epochs, but it was followed more or less instinctively, unconsciously. Finally it was lost in order that men might seek it out of their own impulse, their own freedom. This path must now be sought in its full consciousness.

The transition through which mankind had to pass after the middle of the fifteenth century is what might be called the materialistic test of mankind. If we observe the character of this materialistic period and the development of culture of the last three or four centuries right up to our time, we shall see that this materialistic wave has most intensively and quite particularly taken hold of teacher training. Nothing could have such a lasting effect as the permeation of educational philosophy by materialism. We only need to look at certain details in present-day education to appreciate the great difficulties in the way of progress. Those who today consider themselves well-versed in the problems of education say again and again that all instruction, even in the lowest grades, must be in the form of object lessons. In the teaching of arithmetic, for instance, mechanical aids to calculating are introduced. The greatest value is placed upon having the child see everything first, and then form his own inner concepts about it. To be sure, the urge for such objectivity in education is in many respects fully justified. Nevertheless it raises the question, what becomes of a child if he only receives object lessons? He becomes psychically dried up; the inner dynamic forces of his soul gradually die out. His whole being unites with the objective surroundings, and what should sprout from his inmost soul is gradually deadened. The way material is presented in much of our education today is connected with this deadening of the soul. People do not realize that one kills the soul, but it really happens. And the consequence is what we experience with people today. How many are problem-laden personalities! How many are unable in their

65

later years to produce out of their own inner resources that which could give them consolation and hope in difficult times and enable them to cope with the vicissitudes of life! We see at present many shattered natures. At important moments we ourselves are doubtful as to the direction we should take.

All this is connected with the deficiencies in our educational system, particularly in teacher training. What then do we have to strive for in order to have the right teacher training in future? The fact that a teacher knows the answers to what is asked in his examinations is a secondary matter, for he is mostly asked questions for which he could prepare himself by looking them up in a handbook. The examiners pay no attention to the general soul-attitude of the teacher, and that is what constantly has to pass from him to his students. There is a great difference between teachers as they enter a classroom. When one steps through the door the students feel a certain soul-relationship with him; when another enters they often feel no such relationship at all, but, on the contrary, they feel a chasm between them and are indifferent to him. This expresses itself in a variety of ways, even to ridiculing and sneering at him. All these nuances frequently lead to ruining any real instruction and education.

The burning question, therefore, is, how can teacher training be transformed in future? It can be transformed in only one way, and that is, that the teacher himself absorb what can come from spiritual science as knowledge of man's true nature. The teacher must be permeated by the reality of man's connection with the supersensible worlds. He

66

must be in the position to see in the growing child evidence that he has descended from the supersensible world through conception and birth, has clothed himself with a body, and wishes to acquire here in the physical world what he cannot acquire in the life between death and a new birth, and in which the teacher has to help.

Every child should stand before the soul of the teacher as a question posed by the supersensible world to the sense world. This question cannot be asked in a definite and comprehensive way in regard to every individual child unless one employs the knowledge that comes from spiritual science concerning the nature of man. In the course of the last three or four centuries we gradually acquired the habit of observing man only in regard to his outer, bodily constitution, physiologically. This concept is detrimental, most of all for the educator. It will, therefore, be necessary above everything else for an anthropology resulting from anthroposophy to become the basis for education in the future. This, however, can only happen if man is considered from the points of view we have frequently touched upon here, that characterize him in many respects as a threefold being. But one must make up one's mind to grasp this threefoldness with penetrating insight. From various aspects I have drawn your attention to the fact that man as he confronts us is, first, a man of nerves and senses; popularly expressed he is a head-man. As a second member we have seen, externally, that part in which the rhythmical processes take place, the chest-man; and thirdly, connected with the entire metabolism is the limb-man, metabolic man. What man is as an active being is externally brought to completion in the physical configuration of these three members of his whole organism:

> Head-man, or nerve-sense man;
> Chest-man, or rhythmical man;
> Limb-man, or metabolic man.

It is important to understand the differences between these three members, but this is very uncomfortable for people today because they love diagrams. If one says that man consists of head-man, chest-man, limb-man, he would like to make a line here at the neck, and what is above it is head-man. Likewise, he would like to draw a line in order to limit the chest-man, and so he would have the three members neatly arranged, side by side. Whatever cannot be arranged in such a scheme is just of no interest to modern man.

But this does not correspond to reality. Reality does not make such outlines. To be sure, man above the shoulders is chiefly head-man, nerve-sense man, but he is not only that. The sense of touch and the sense of warmth, for instance, are spread over the whole body, so that the head-system permeates the entire organism. Thus one can say, the human head is chiefly head. The chest is less head but still somewhat head. The limbs and everything belonging to the metabolic system are still less head, but nevertheless head. One really has to say that the whole human being is head, but only the head is chiefly head. The chest-man is not only in the chest; he is chiefly expressed, of course, in those organs where the rhythms of the heart and breathing are most definitely shown. But breathing also extends into the head; and the blood circulation in its rhythm continues on into the head and limbs.

So we can say that our way of thinking is inclined to place these things side by side, and in this we see how little our concepts are geared to outer reality. For here things merge; and we have to realize that if we separate head, chest, and metabolic man we must think them together again. We must never think them as separated but always think them together again. A person who wishes only to think things separated resembles a man who wishes only to inhale, never to exhale.

Here you have something that teachers in future will have to do; they must quite specially acquire for themselves this inwardly mobile thinking, this unschematic thinking. For only by doing so can their soul forces approach reality. A person will not come near to reality if he is unable to conceive of approaching it from a larger point of view, as a phenomenon of the age. One has to overcome the tendency to be content with investigating life in its details, a tendency that has been growing in scientific studies. Instead one must see these details in connection with the great questions of life.

One question will become important for the entire evolution of spiritual culture in future, namely, the question of immortality. We must become clear about the way a great part of humanity conceives of immortality, particularly since the time when many have come to a complete denial of it. What lives in most people today who, still on the basis of customary religion, want to be informed about immortality? In these people there lives the urge to know something about what becomes of the soul when it has passed through the portal of death.

If we ask about the interest men take in the question of the eternity of man's essential being, we come to no other answer than this, that the main interest they have is connected with man's concern about what happens to him when he passes through death. Man is conscious of being an ego. In this ego his thinking, feeling, and willing live. The idea that this ego might be annihilated is unbearable to him. Above all then he is interested in the possibility of carrying the ego through death, and in what happens to it afterward. Most religious systems, in speaking about immortality, chiefly bear in mind this same question: What becomes of the human soul when man passes through death?

Now you must feel that the question of immortality, put in this manner, takes on an extraordinarily egotistical character. Basically it is an egotistical urge that arouses man's interest in knowing what happens to him when he passes through death. If men of the present age would practice more self-knowledge, take counsel with themselves, and not surrender to illusions as they do now, they would realize the strong part egotism plays in the interest they have in knowing something about the destiny of the soul after death.

This kind of feeling has become especially strong in the last three to four centuries when the trials of materialism have come upon us. What has thus taken hold of human souls as a habit of thought and feeling cannot be overcome through abstract theories or doctrines. But must it remain so? Is it necessary that only the egotist in human nature speak when the question of the eternal core of man's being is raised?

When we consider everything connected with this problem we must say: The fact that man's soul-mood has developed as we have just indicated stems from the way religions have neglected to observe man as he is born, as he grows into the world from his first cry, as his soul in such miraculous fashion permeates the body more and more; their neglect to observe how in man there gradually develops that part of him which has lived in the spiritual world before birth. How little do people ask today: When man is born, what is it that continues on from the spiritual world into man as a physical being?

In future primary attention will have to be paid to this. We must learn to listen to the revelation of spirit and soul in the growing child as they existed before birth. We must learn to see in him the continuation of his sojourn in the spiritual world. Then our relationship to the eternal core of man's being will become less and less egotistical. For if we are not interested in what continues in physical life from out the spiritual world, if we are only interested in what continues after death, then we are egotistical. But to behold what continues out of the spiritual into physical existence in a certain way lays the basis for an unegotistical mood of soul.

Egotism does not ask about this continuation because it is certain that man exists, and one is satisfied with that fact. But he is uncertain whether he still exists after death, therefore he would like to have this proved. Egotism urges him on to this. But true knowledge does not accrue to man out

71

of egotism, not even out of the sublimated egotism that is interested in the soul's continuation after death. Can one deny that the religions strongly reckon with such egotism? This must be overcome. He who is able to look into the spiritual world knows that from this conquest not only knowledge will result but an entirely different attitude toward one's human environment. We will confront the growing child with completely different feelings when we are aware that here we have the continuation of what could not tarry any longer in the spiritual world.

From this point of view just consider how the following takes on a different aspect. One could say that man was in the spiritual world before he descended into the physical world. Up there he must no longer have been able to find his goal. The spiritual world must have been unable to give to the soul what it strives for. There the urge must have arisen to descend into the physical world, to clothe oneself with a body in order to search in that world for what no longer could be found in the spiritual world as the time of birth approached.

It is a tremendous deepening of life if we adopt such a point of view in our feelings. Whereas the egotistical point of view makes man more and more abstract, theoretical, and inclines him toward head-thinking, the unegotistical point of view urges him to understand the world with love, to lay hold of it through love. This is one of the elements which must be taken up in teacher training; to look at pre-natal man, and not only feel the riddle of death but also the riddle of birth.

Then, however, we must learn to raise anthropology to the

higher level of anthroposophy, by acquiring a feeling for the forms that express themselves in three-membered man. I said recently that the head in its spherical form is, so to say, merely placed on top of the rest of the organism. And the chest-man, he appears as if we could take a piece of the head, enlarge it, and we would have the spine. While the head bears its center within itself, the chest-man has its center at a great distance from itself. If you were to imagine this as a large head, this head then would belong to a man lying on his back. Thus, if we were to consider this spine as an imperfect head we would have a man lying horizontally, and a man standing vertically.

If we consider metabolic man, matters become still more complicated, and it is not possible to draw this in two dimensions. In short, the three members of the human organism, observed as to their plastic form, appear very different from one another. The head, we may say, is a totality; the chest-man is not a totality but a fragment; and metabolic man is much more so.

Now why is it that the human head appears self-enclosed? It is because this head, of all the members of man's organism, is to the greatest degree adapted to the physical world. This may appear strange to you because you are accustomed to consider the human head as the noblest member of man. Yet it is true that this head is to the greatest degree adapted to physical existence. It expresses physical existence in the highest degree. Thus we may say, if we wish to characterize the physical body in its main aspects we must look toward the head. In regard to the head, man is mostly physical body. In regard to the chest organs, the organs of rhythm, man is mostly ether body. In regard to the metabolic organs, he is mostly astral body. The ego has no distinct expression in the physical world as yet.

Here we have arrived at a point of view which is very important to consider. We must say to ourselves, if we look at the human head we see the chief part of the physical body. The head expresses to the highest degree what is manifest in man. In the chest-man the ether body is more active; therefore, physically, the chest of man is less perfect than the head. And metabolic man is still less perfect, because in it the ether body is but little active and the astral body is most active. I have often emphasized that the ego is the baby; as yet it has practically no physical correlate.

So you see we may also describe man in the following way: He consists of the physical body, characterized mostly by the sphere-form of the head; he consists of the ether body, characterized mostly by the chest section; he consists of the astral body, characterized mostly by metabolic man. We can hardly indicate anything for the ego in physical man. Thus, each of the three members—the nerve-sense system, the rhythmic system, the metabolic system—becomes an image of something standing behind it: The head the image for the physical body; the chest for the ether body; metabolism for the astral body. We must learn to observe this, not in the manner of research clinics where a corpse is investigated and no attention is paid to the question of whether a piece of tissue belongs to the chest or the head. We must learn to realize that head, chest, and metabolic man have different relationships to the cosmos and express in picture form different principles standing behind them. This will extend the present anthropological mode of observation into the anthropomorphic one. Observed purely physically, chest and head organs have equal value. Whether you dissect the lung or the brain, from the physical aspect both are matter. From the spiritual aspect, however, this is by no means the case. If you dissect the brain you have it quite distinctly before you. If you dissect the chest, let us say the lungs, you have them quite indistinctly before you, because the ether body plays its important role in the chest while man is asleep.

What I have just discussed has its spiritual counter-image. One who has advanced through meditation, through the exercises described in our literature, gradually comes to the point where he really experiences man in his three members. You know that I speak of this threefold membering from a certain point of view in the chapter of my book, *Knowledge of the Higher Worlds and Its Attainment,* where I indicate the Guardian of the Threshold. But one can also bring about a picture of this three-membering through strong concentration upon one's self, by separating head-man, chest-man, and metabolic-man. Then one will notice what it is that makes the head into this head we have. If through inner concentration we withdraw the head from its appendage, the rest of the organism, and have it before us without the influence of the other members, the head is dead; it is no longer alive. It is impossible, clair-voyantly, to separate the head from the rest of the organism without perceiving it as a corpse. With the chest-system this is possible; it remains alive. And if you separate the astral body by separating the metabolic system, it runs

75

away from you. The astral body does not remain in its place, it follows the cosmic movements.

Now imagine you stand before a child with the knowledge I have just developed for you, and you look at him in an unbiased way. You observe his head, how it carries death in itself. You look at the influence of the chest upon the head; it comes alive. You see the child as he starts to walk. You notice that it is the astral body that is active in walking. Now the child becomes something inwardly transparent to you. The head—a corpse; the outspreading life in him when he stands still, is quiet. The moment he begins to walk you notice that it is the astral body that walks. Man can walk because this astral body uses up substances in moving, metabolism is active in a certain way. How can we observe the ego?—for everything now has been exhausted, so to say. You observe the head-man, the life-giving element of the chest-man, the walking. What remains by which we might observe the ego externally? I have already stated that the ego hardly has an external correlate. You can see the ego only if you observe a child in his increasing growth. At one year he is very little; at two he is bigger, and so on. As you connect your impressions of him year after year, then join in your mind what he is in the successive years, you see the ego physically. You never see the ego in a child if you merely confront him, but only when you see him grow. If men would not surrender to illusions but see reality they would be aware of the fact that when they meet a person they cannot physically perceive his ego, only when they observe him in the various periods of his life. If you

76

meet a man again after twenty years you will perceive his ego vividly in the change that has taken place in him; especially if twenty years ago you saw him as a child.

Now I beg you not to ponder just theoretically what I have said. I ask you to enliven your thoughts and consider this when you observe man: Head—corpse; chest—vitalization; the astral body in walking; the ego through growing. Thus the whole man comes alive who previously confronted you like a wax doll. For what is it that we ordinarily see of man with our physical eyes and our intellect? A wax doll! It comes alive if you add what I have just described.

In order to do this you need to have your perception permeated by what spiritual science can pour into your feelings, into your relationship to the world. A walking child discloses to you the astral body. The gesture of his walking —every child walks differently—stems from the configuration of his astral body. Growth expresses something of the ego.

Here karma works strongly in man. As an example somewhat removed from our present age, take Johann Gottlieb Fichte. I have characterized him for you from various aspects, as a great philosopher, as a Bolshevist, and so on. Now let us look at him from another point of view, imagining him as he passed us by on the street and we watched him as he went. We would see a man, stocky, not very tall. What does the manner in which he has grown, disclose? He is stunted. He puts his feet, heels first, firmly on the ground. The whole Fichte-ego expresses itself in this. Not a detail of the man do we miss when we observe him so—his growth stunted by hunger in his youth, stocky, putting his heels down firmly. We could hear the manner of his speech by observing him in this way from behind.

You see, a spiritual element can enter into the externalities of life, but this does not occur unless men change their attitude. For people today such observation of their fellowmen might be an evil indiscretion, and it would not be very desirable if this were to spread. People have been so influenced by ever-growing materialism that they, for instance, refrain from opening letters that do not belong to them only because it is prohibited; otherwise they would do it. With such an attitude things cannot change. But the more we grow toward the future the more must we learn to take in spiritually what surrounds us in the sense world. The start must be made with the pedagogical activity of the teacher in regard to the growing child. Physiognomic pedagogy; the will to solve the greatest riddle, MAN, in every single individual, through education.

Now you can feel how strong is the test for mankind in our times. What I have discussed here really presses forward toward individualization, toward the consideration of every human being as an entity in himself. As a great ideal the thought must hover before us that no one person duplicates another; every single individual is a being in himself. Unless we learn to acknowledge that everyone is an entity in himself mankind will not attain its goal on earth. But how far removed we are today from the attitude that strives for this goal! We level human beings down. We do not test them in regard to their individual qualities. Hermann Bahr, of whom I have often spoken to you, disclosed once how the education of our times tends to do away with individualization. He participated in the social life of the 1890's in Berlin, and one evening at a dinner party he was seated of course with one lady at his right, another at his left. The next evening he sat again between two ladies, but only from the place cards could he gather that they were two different ladies. He did not look at them very attentively because, after all, the lady of yesterday and the lady of today did not look any different. What he saw in them was exactly the same. The culture of society, and especially of industry, makes every human being appear the same, externally, not permitting the individuality to emerge. Thus, present-day man strives for leveling, whereas the inmost goal of man must be his striving for individualization. We cover up individuality, whereas it is most important to seek it.

In his instruction the teacher must begin to direct his insight toward the individuality. Teacher training has to be permeated by an attitude which strives to find the individuality in men. This can only come about through an enlivening of our thoughts about man as I have described it. We must really become conscious of the fact that it is not a mechanism that moves one forward, but the astral body; it pulls the physical body along. Compare what thus can arise in your souls as an inwardly enlivened and mobile image of the whole human being, with what ordinary science offers today—a homunculus, a veritable homunculus! Science says nothing about man, it preaches the homunculus. The real human being above everything else must come into pedagogy, for now he is completely outside of it.

The question of education is a question of teacher training, and as long as this fact is not recognized nothing fruitful can come into education. You see, from a higher point of view things so belong together that one can make a true connection between them. Today one strives to develop man's activities as subjects side by side. A student learns anthropology, he learns about religion; the subjects have nothing to do with each other. In fact, as you have seen, what one observes about man borders on the question of immortality, of the eternal essence of human nature. We had to link this question to one's immediate perception of man. It is this mobility of soul experience which must enter education. Then, inner faculties quite different from those developed today in teacher training schools will come into being. This is of great importance.

Today I wished to put before you the fact that the science of the spirit must permeate everything, and that without it the great social problems of the present time cannot be solved.

V

Dornach, August 16, 1919

In THE observations we are making here we have to enter more and more into the history of the age and see how cosmic forces work into the evolution of the present time and form the foundations of our human life. You have seen from our discussions yesterday that it becomes increasingly necessary to transform the rigid, abstract concepts one is accustomed to at present into flowing, mobile, living concepts if mankind is to progress. A special light is thrown upon all the facts in question by that soul force we call intelligence. The man of the present is particularly proud of his intelligence. He considers the gradual acquisition of intelligence a special mark of distinction.

If man today looks back into earlier epochs when people had pictorial thoughts, he considers their constitution of spirit and soul in that time childlike. He believes that only through his intelligence and his science can one acquire a correct knowledge of what people in earlier periods of evolution tried to comprehend through myths and legends. He looks back to those childlike stages of evolution and is very proud of having come so far, especially in the development of intelligence. Now let us consider the special characteristics of human intelligence, that soul force in which modern man takes such pride. If we speak today of intelligence we refer to a soul force of which we have a definite concept and cannot imagine it to be different. People of former epochs, however, also had intelligence, but of a different sort. If we wish to become fully acquainted with the significance of so-called intelligence for modern man, we must ask: What was the nature of former intelligence, and how did it gradually change into the intelligence of our time?

Today we shall not go back further than the third post-Atlantean period, the Egypto-Chaldean, followed by the Greco-Latin, which in turn was followed by our own. We shall consider the peculiarity of the intelligence of these ancient peoples and then pass over to the special kind of intelligence that we of the fifth post-Atlantean epoch possess. You see from this that I assume it is not correct to think intelligence is intelligence, that only one kind is possible; that whoever has our intelligence is intelligent, and whoever does not have it is un-intelligent. This is not correct. Intelligence passes through metamorphoses and transforms itself. In the Egypto-Chaldean period it was different from today. This can best be described by saying, those people felt and comprehended instinctively, through their intelligence, their relationship to the entire cosmos. The Egyptians and Chaldeans thought very little, or not at all, about what modern man thinks by means of his intelligence. When they brought their intelligence into play their connection with the cosmos lived in it. They knew their relationship to this or that zodiacal constellation; they knew what kind of influence moon, sun, and planets had upon man's soul and bodily constitutions. They knew the influence of the course of the seasons upon him. All this they grasped through their intelligence. They acquired an entirely inward picture of their relationship with the cosmos.

This intelligence had become transformed by the time the Egypto-Chaldean period came to an end in the eighth century B.C. The connection with the cosmos was no longer the vital experience it had been prior to this time. It lived like an echo, a kind of memory in human souls. In its place there entered into the Greek intelligence man's reflecting on himself as an earth dweller, how he is related to the cosmos. But the Greek had a certain feeling in using his intelligence. He understood everything of the earthly world that is subject to death. He knew that if he wanted to comprehend the supersensible he had to turn to that power of perception which still existed atavistically in the pre-Christian era. Through reflection, through intelligence, he learned to know the laws which underlie all that dies on earth. Said the pupils of Plato: "If I want to understand the living I must *see;* by merely thinking I only grasp what is dead."

In the Greek mystery schools something quite definite in this connection was explained. It was about like this: Everything is spiritual; spiritual processes and laws also underlie what seems to be material. There are spiritual laws that concern you in so far as you have a body. When you pass through the portal of death your body is delivered to the material powers and substances of the earth. But these powers and substances are only apparently material. They too are spiritual, but they are permeated by that spiritual force which appears to you as death. If with your intelligence you grasp any kind of laws, you see that these are the laws of death. They are the laws that are active in graves, in corpses. If you want to know the nature of the spiritual powers in which you live here on earth, or in the body-free state between death and a new birth—thus spoke the mystery teacher to his pupils—then you must be convinced of that which you *see*. If you are not so convinced, concepts and ideas developed only through your intelligence will merely grasp the spirit in matter, in your physical body.

Whereas the Egypto-Chaldean felt and perceived in his intelligence his relationship to the entire cosmos, the Greek perceived through his intelligence what governs the tomb. We, too, only perceive through our intelligence what governs the tomb; however, we are not conscious of it. So we go to the dissecting laboratories, investigate the corpse, and consider the laws of the corpse that we grasp through our intelligence to be the laws of man. Yet, they are only the laws of the grave.

But again, since the middle of the fifteenth century, a gradual transformation of intelligence is taking place. Although it is still very much like that of the Greeks it is undergoing a transformation, and we are in the beginning of it. In the coming centuries and millennia this intelligence will become something very, very different. Even today it shows a tendency toward what will come in future, a tendency

84

merely to grasp what is error, untruth, deception; a tendency to ponder only what is evil.

The mystery pupils and especially the initiates had known for some time that human intelligence approaches its development toward evil, and that it becomes more and more impossible to recognize the good through mere intelligence. Mankind finds itself today within this transition. We may say, it is still barely possible, if men exert their intelligence and do not bear especially wild instincts in themselves, to look toward the light of what is good. But human intelligence will more and more develop the inclination to plan evil, to bring error into knowledge, and insert evil into man's moral life.

This is one of the reasons initiates called themselves men of anxiety. Indeed, if one observes the evolution of mankind from this aspect as I have just done, it causes anxiety, precisely because of the way intelligence is developing. It is not for nothing that it fills modern man with pride and haughtiness. This is the pre-taste of intelligence becoming evil in the fifth post-Atlantean age, which is beginning now. If man were not to develop anything else but intelligence he would become an evil being on earth. If we want to think of a wholesome future for mankind we must not count on the one-sided development of intelligence. In Egypt and Chaldea it was good; later it entered into a relationship with the forces of death; and it will enter into a relationship with the forces of error, deception, and evil.

This is something about which mankind should have no illusions. In an unbiased fashion humanity should reckon with the fact that it has to protect itself against this one-sided development of intelligence. It is not in vain that precisely through the anthroposophically oriented science of the spirit another element will be added by taking in what can be gained through a renewed perception of the spiritual world. This cannot be grasped by intelligence, but only if we take into ourselves what the science of initiation brings down from the spiritual world through vision.

But something quite objective is necessary here. At this point we confront a deep secret of Christian-esoteric development. If the Mystery of Golgotha had not taken place in the course of earth evolution human beings could not avoid gradually becoming evil through their intelligence; inevitably they would fall prey to error. You know that with the Mystery of Golgotha there flowed into mankind's evolution not merely a doctrine, a theory, a world view, a religion, but a real fact. In the man Jesus of Nazareth there lived the extraterrestrial being, the Christ. Through the fact that the Christ dwelt in Jesus of Nazareth, when Jesus died the Christ-being passed over into earthly evolution. He is within it. We must only be conscious that this is an objective fact which has nothing to do with what we know or feel subjectively. We must know it for the sake of knowledge; we must take it up into our ethical culture for the sake of our morality. The Christ-being has flowed into mankind's evolution. He is within it since the resurrection. He dwells especially in our soul forces. Take this fact in its full depth!

Look at the difference between men who lived before the Mystery of Golgotha and those who lived after it. Certainly

they are the same people, because souls pass through repeated earth lives. But we must differentiate between those
who lived before this Mystery and those who lived after it.
A general concept of God is not the Christ concept. We can
arrive at a general concept of God if we observe nature in
her phenomena, if we observe physical man, externally. The
Christ-being is of such a nature that we can only come near
it if, in the course of earthly life, we uncover something in
ourselves. We can find the general concept of God by simply
saying: We have come into existence out of the forces of the
world. The Christ concept we must find in ourselves by
advancing beyond the phenomena in nature. If, living in
the world, we do not find the concept of God, this is a kind
of sickness. A healthy human being is never really athe-
istic. If he is, he must be bodily or psychically sick in some
way, and the illness expresses itself in atheism.

To be unable to recognize the Christ is not an illness but
a misfortune, the neglecting of an opportunity offered by
life. By reflecting upon our having been born out of nature
and its forces, and pursuing this thought with a healthy
soul, we may arrive at a concept of God. By experiencing
in the course of our life something like a re-birth we may
arrive at a concept of Christ. Birth leads to God; re-birth
to Christ. This re-birth, through which Christ as a Being
may be found in man, could not be attained prior to the
Mystery of Golgotha. This is the difference upon which I
wish you to focus your attention. Prior to the Mystery of
Golgotha man could not yet experience this re-birth, could
not yet recognize that Christ lives in him, because the Christ-
being had not yet flowed into mankind. After the Mystery

of Golgotha man can recognize Him. He can find the spark of Christ in himself if he exerts himself in the way he lives.

In this re-birth, this finding of the Christ-spark in oneself, in being able to say sincerely and honestly to oneself, "Not I but the Christ in me," lies the possibility of preventing the intellect from falling prey to deception and evil. And this, in the esoteric Christian sense, is the higher concept of redemption. We must develop our intelligence, for we must not become un-intelligent; but in striving to develop it we are faced with the temptation to fall into error and evil. We can escape this temptation only if we acquire a feeling for what the Mystery of Golgotha has brought into mankind's evolution.

It is already so, that man in his consciousness of Christ, in his union with Christ, can find the possibility of escaping evil and error. The man of Egypt and Chaldea did not need re-birth in Christ because he still felt his relationship with the cosmos through his natural intelligence. The Greek faced the seriousness of death when he surrendered to his intelligence. Now mankind lives at the beginning of an age in which intelligence would become evil if human souls would not let themselves be permeated by the Christ-power. This is a very serious matter. It shows how certain things that proclaim themselves in our time have to be taken; how we have to be aware that in our age men acquire the aptitude for evil precisely because they approach a higher development of their intelligence. It would of course be entirely wrong to believe that we should suppress intelligence. It must not be suppressed. But for the person with insight a certain courage will be needed in future in surrendering to intelligence, because it tempts one to evil and error; and because, in the permeation of intelligence with the Christ-principle, we must find the possibility of transforming intelligence. It would become completely Ahrimanic if the Christ-principle were not to permeate human souls.

You see how much of what I have just characterized is already coming to light, which is perceptible to a person with insight. As you think about it, just notice how many cruelties permeate our culture, cruelties with which the cruelties of barbarian times cannot be compared. If you consider this you will hardly doubt that the dawn of the decline in intelligence is proclaiming itself. One should not look superficially at the so-called cultural phenomena of our age. Nor should one doubt that modern men have to arouse themselves to a real comprehension of the Christ-impulse if evolution is to go forward in a healthy way. Two evidences of this can be definitely seen today: People who are very intelligent and have a decided inclination toward evil; and many others who subconsciously suppress but do not fight this inclination toward evil, merely letting their intelligence sleep. Drowsiness of the soul; or, with wakeful souls, a strong inclination toward evil and error—this may be observed at present.

Now remember what I said to you here one evening before my last journey, how different children are who were born within the last five to eight years, from those born some decades earlier. They have a trace of melancholy in their faces which is clearly discernible. This comes from the fact that souls today do not gladly descend into this world so filled with materialism. One might say that the souls have a certain fear and reluctance to enter the world in which intelligence is inclined toward evil and is in a declining development.

This also is something future educators and teachers must take into their consciousness. Children today are different from those of some decades ago. Even superficial observation shows this clearly. One has to educate and teach them differently from previous times. One must teach out of awareness that one has to bring about a salvation in the case of every individual child; that one has to steer him toward finding the Christ-impulse in the course of his life, toward finding a re-birth within himself.

Such things must not live in the teacher as mere theory; they can be introduced into one's teaching only if one is strongly taken hold of by them in one's own soul. It must be demanded of teachers especially that their souls be strongly gripped by the anxiety that arises in confronting the temptation the intellect offers. The pride that man takes today in his intellect might indeed take its revenge if it were not checked by his being consciously able to say, strongly and energetically, "The best in me as a human being of this and following incarnations is what I find in myself as the Christ-impulse."

We must, however, be clear that this Christ-impulse must not be the dogmatism of some religious body. Since the middle of the fifteenth century religious communities, instead of bringing the Christ-impulse close to mankind, have contributed to its alienation. The religious bodies pretend this or that, but in doing so they do not bring the Christ-impulse near to man. It is necessary for a person to feel that everything in relation to the Mystery of Golgotha which can reveal itself to his inmost being is connected with what has come into the earth through that Mystery. If we experience the true meaning of the earth as inherent in that Mystery, then we must bring ourselves to say: The evolution of the earth would be meaningless if man were to fall prey through his intelligence to evil and error. Thus, if we feel wherein the real meaning of earth evolution actually lies, we also feel that this evolution would be senseless without the Mystery of Golgotha.

We must permeate ourselves through and through with this conviction if, today and in future, we wish to do something toward man's education and instruction. We require these comprehensive points of view. But you know how far people are today from such views. Therefore, nothing is more necessary than to point again and again not only to the importance of spiritual scientific teaching, but to the seriousness that must take hold of our souls through our learning to know through spiritual science the pertinent facts in the evolution of mankind. For not only our knowledge but our whole life is to receive an impulse through spiritual science. Without our feeling this seriousness we are not true scientists of the spirit.

I beg you to pay close attention to this particular revelation out of spiritual science: That human intelligence, left to itself, travels on the path toward the Ahrimanic; that it can become active for the good only through taking in the true Christ-impulse. I believe that whoever takes the full seriousness of this truth into himself will also carry the same seriousness into the relationship he forms to the various world concepts and movements of the present time. Here there is much to be done.

People who have recently come from the East of Europe tell with great horror of a fact that indeed does not testify to an advance on the path toward civilization. I refer to the coming into existence of the so-called "gun-women." This is a special class of people, women of the East-European population, who are being used in the present revolutionary movements. In certain regions of the East young women are chosen and equipped with guns left over from the war, and their task is to shoot those people who are opposing the government in power. These female gunmen are dressed up in stolen finery and take their pleasure in carrying guns and shooting people. They consider it to be in tune with modern attitudes to brag about the fine feeling they have gradually acquired for the way the blood of young people spurts out, and how the blood of older people looks. In truth, we have arrived at a quite special configuration of our modern civilization! For the institution of gun-women is a development of the present age.

We have to point to such phenomena. They make us see the counterpart of the seriousness of our age. Of course, we need not know of these abominable excesses in our so-called progressive culture in order really to feel this seriousness which calls upon us for devoted attention to it at the present time. Such seriousness arises in us out of knowing the evolution of mankind itself. One could wish that the sleep which has taken hold of modern man may pass over into an awakening. The most worthy awakening can only consist in being gripped by the earnestness of the task given to humanity, and by seeing the danger of the intellect being one-sidedly left to itself and moving in an Ahrimanic direction. This should be the force permeating us with such earnestness.

VI

Dornach, August 17, 1919

WHAT I said yesterday about the path of the human intellect toward the future, rests upon definite facts that can be brought to light through spiritual-scientific knowledge. Today we shall deal with some of these facts. You must be conscious in a practical way, I might say, of the following.

When a man confronts you he is that being we speak about in spiritual science. That is to say, above everything we must always be aware that he is a four-membered being, as you know from my book *Theosophy*. We have before us the ego, the astral body, ether body, and physical body. The fact that every time a person stands before us we are confronted by these four members of the human entity, brings it about that ordinary human perception does not know what it faces in man. Ordinarily one thinks: "What I see before me, filling space, is the physical body." But what is physical in it we would not see as we usually see it if it were to confront us merely as physical body. We see it as it usually is today only because it is permeated by the ether body, the astral body, and ego. Strange as it may sound, that which is the physical body proper is a corpse, even during our lifetime. When we are confronted by a human corpse we are actually confronted by the physical body. In the corpse we have physical man not permeated by ether and astral body and ego. It is forsaken by them and shows its true nature. You do not visualize yourself properly if you believe you carry what you consider to be the physical body of man with you through space. A more correct view would be if you thought of yourself as a corpse with your ego, astral and etheric bodies carrying this corpse through space.

A consciousness of the true nature of man's being becomes more and more important for our age. For the conditions existing in the present cycle of mankind's evolution were not the same in earlier periods. What I am now relating cannot be ascertained by outer physical science, but spiritual-scientific cognition does observe these facts. As you know, the fourth post-Atlantean age begins in the eighth century B.C.; further back we come to the Egypto-Chaldean period. At that time human bodies had a constitution different from that of today. Those you find now in the museum as mummies had a much more delicate constitution than present-day human bodies. They were much more permeated by the plant element; they were not so completely corpse as is the modern human body. As physical bodies they were akin to plant nature, whereas the present-day physical body, since the Greco-Latin age, is akin to the mineral world. If through some cosmic miracle the bodies of that ancient population were to be bestowed upon us, we would all be ill. We would carry proliferating

95

growths in our body. Many a disease consists in the fact that the human body atavistically returns to conditions that were the normal ones in the Egypto-Chaldean age. Today we find tumorous formations in the body which are caused by the fact that a part of this or that person's body develops the tendency to become what the whole body was for the ancient Egypto-Chaldean population.

This is closely connected with human evolution. We as modern men carry a corpse in our body. The ancient Egyptian carried as his body something of a plant-like nature. The result was that his knowledge was different from ours, his intelligence acted differently. What do we know through our science that we are so proud of? Only that which is dead. Science shows that life cannot be grasped with ordinary intelligence. To be sure, certain research scientists believe that if they continue with their chemical experiments the moment will come when they will be able, through complicated combinations of atoms, molecules, and their interactions, to know the processes of life. This moment will never come. On the chemico-physical path one will only be able to grasp the minerally dead; that is to say, one will only grasp that aspect of the living which is a corpse.

Yet, what in man is intelligent and gains knowledge is nevertheless this physical body, this corpse. What then does this corpse do as we carry it about? It achieves most in a knowledge of mathematics and geometry. Everything is transparent there. The further we move from the mathematical-geometrical the more un-transparent do matters become. The reason for this is that the human corpse is the real knower today; the dead can only recognize the dead.

Today what the ether body is, the astral body, the ego, does not think in man; it remains in obscurity. If the ether body would be able to know in the same way that the physical body knows the dead, it would know the life of the plant world. This was the peculiar thing with the Egyptian, that with his plant-like, living body he had knowledge of the plant world in a way quite different from ours. Much instinctive knowledge of the plant world can be traced back to what was embodied in Egyptian culture through their instinctively knowing consciousness. Even what is known today in botany about substances for medicinal use comes often from traditions originating in ancient Egyptian wisdom. You know how a number of so-called lodges, not founded on genuine fundamentals, call themselves Egyptian lodges. That is because they refer back to Egypt if they want to impart certain knowledge—which, however, is no longer very valuable. In these circles there still live certain traditions stemming from the wisdom which could be had through the Egyptian body. One can say, as humanity gradually progresses into the Greco-Latin period the living, human plant-body gradually died out. We carry an extremely dead body in us; especially is this true for the head. The science of the initiates perceives the human head as a corpse, as something continually dying. More and more will humanity become conscious of the fact that its vehicle for knowledge is a corpse; that it therefore knows only what is dead.

For this reason, the further we go into the future the more intensively will we feel a longing to know what is living. But the living will not be known through ordinary intelligence bound to the corpse. Much will be needed to make it possible for man again to penetrate the world in a living way. We must know today what it is that man has lost. When he passed over from the Atlantean to the post-Atlantean age there was much he could not do that he can do today. Since a certain time in your childhood you are able to say "I" in referring to yourself. You may say it without any great respect. But in former ages of mankind's evolution this "I" was not referred to with so little respect. There were times, prior to the Egyptian age, when a name for "I" was used which, when pronounced, stupefied a person. Pronouncing it, therefore, was avoided. If people right after the Atlantean epoch had experienced the pronouncing of the name for "I"—at that time it was only known to the initiates—the whole congregation would have fainted, so powerful was the effect of uttering this name for "I." An echo of this fact lingered with the ancient Hebrews who spoke of the unutterable name of the Deity in the soul; a word which only the initiates were permitted to speak, or that was expressed before the congregation in a kind of eurythmy.

The ineffable name of God had its origin in what I have just told you. Gradually this fact was lost, and the deep effect of such practices diminished. In the first post-Atlantean epoch a deep effect in the ego; in the second epoch a deep effect in the astral body; in the third epoch a deep effect in the ether body, but the effect was bearable—an effect which, as I stated yesterday, brought men into connection with the cosmos. Today we can say "I"—we can say anything—without its having a deep effect upon us, because we grasp the world with our corpse. That is to say, we grasp what is dead, what is mineral in the world. But we must arouse ourselves to rise again to those regions in which we can take hold of the living. Whereas the Greco-Latin period created more and more dead knowledge for the corpse, in our time intelligence follows the path I mentioned yesterday. We must, therefore, resist mere intelligence; we must add something to it. It is in the nature of our time that we have to retrace the path of development, so that in the fifth post-Atlantean period we learn to know the plant, in the sixth period the animal, and in the seventh the truly human. Thus it will be our present task to pass beyond a knowledge of the mineral and learn to know the plant element.

Now after realizing this, ask yourself who is the person who exemplifies this search for plant knowledge. It is Goethe. Contrary to the preoccupation of all outer science with what is dead, he occupied himself with the life, the growth, the metamorphosis of plants. Thus he was the man of the fifth post-Atlantean period in its elementary beginnings. In his small treatise of the year 1790, *An Attempt to Explain the Metamorphosis of Plants,* you will see how Goethe tries to comprehend the plant from leaf to leaf as something developing, unfolding, not as something completed, dead. That is the beginning of the knowledge that should be sought in the fifth post-Atlantean epoch.

In Goetheanism we have the keynote for this. Science will have to wake up in the Goethean sense, will have to pass from the dead to the living. This is what is meant when I say again and again that we must acquire the ability to leave behind the dead, abstract concepts and arrive at those that are living and concrete. What I said two days ago and yesterday is basically the way to these living, concrete concepts.

It will not be possible to enter into these concepts and ideas if we are not ready to develop our general world view and concept of life as a unity. Through the special configuration of our culture we are forced to let the various currents of our world view run side by side in a disorganized fashion. Just think how man's religious view of the world and his scientific view often run parallel, completely disconnected. He builds no bridge between the two; indeed, he is afraid of doing so. We must make it clear that this state of affairs cannot continue.

I have drawn your attention to the egotistical way man forms his world view at the present time. I have described how men today are chiefly interested in the life of the soul after death. This interest springs from pure egotism. I have said we must pass on to interest in the life of the soul from birth onward, seeing it as a continuation of the life prior to birth. If we were to observe the child's growth into the world as a continuation of his pre-natal existence, with the same concern we feel for his soul after death, our thinking about the world would be much less egotistical than it is today. But this egotism in our world view is connected with many other things.

Here I come to a point where men today must become ever more clear about underlying facts. In the period of time culminating in our age the egotistic element was chiefly developed. The ego has permeated man's viewing of the world; it has also permeated his will. We must not deceive ourselves about that. The religious denominations in particular have become egotistical. This you can see even in externalities. Just consider how modern preachers have to reckon with people's egotism. The more they make promises concerning the life of the soul after death the more they reach their goal. People today have little interest in other spiritual questions; in, for instance, that creative flow of life which shows itself so wonderfully after birth in the soul that previously was in the spiritual world.

A result of this lack of interest is the way man thinks about the Divine in the various religious denominations. The fact that we visualize a God as The Highest has no special meaning. Here it is essential that we free ourselves from deception. What do most people mean today if they say "God"? What kind of being do people refer to when they speak of God? It is an Angel; nothing else but their own Angel whom they call God. People have just a bare intimation that a protective spirit guides their life; they look up to him and call him their God. This is the egotism of the churches, that they do not pass beyond the Angel with their concept of God. A narrowing of interests is caused by egotism; and this narrowing of interests is to be clearly seen in public life.

Do people today ask about the general destiny of mankind? Oh! it is often very sad if one wants to speak to people about human destiny. No one has any idea of the degree of change that has taken place in this respect in a comparatively short time. Today we may say to people: The military conflict that has spread over the earth during the last four or five years will be followed by the mightiest spiritual battle, which will cover the earth in a form never experienced before. Its origin lies in the fact of the Occident naming as *illusion* or *ideology* what the Orient calls *reality,* and the Orient feeling as *reality* what the Occident calls *ideology.* We may draw people's attention to this weighty matter and it does not even dawn on them that if something similar had been said only a hundred years ago it would have so taken hold of people's souls that they would never have gotten over it.

This change in humanity, this growing indifference to the great questions of destiny, is the most striking phenomenon. Everything bounces off mankind, so to say. The most comprehensive, incisive facts are accepted like a sensation. People are not deeply shaken by them. The reason for this is the clever, ever increasing egotism that constricts men's interests. We may have whatever fine democracies where men meet in parliaments, but concern for the fate of mankind does not permeate them, because the people who are elected to these parliaments do not feel the urgency to know mankind's destiny. Egotistical interests hold sway. Everyone has his own egotistical interest. Similarities in outer interests such as often arise from one's profession, lead people to form groups. When the groups are large enough, majorities arise. In this way a concern not for human destinies but only for egotism, multiplied by the number of persons involved, becomes active in parliaments and men's proposals.

Because of the way egotism lives in people now, even their religious professions are under its influence. They will have their necessary renewal if people's interests broaden; that is, if men will again look beyond their personal destiny to the destiny of mankind; if they will be deeply moved when one tells them that in the West a culture develops that is different from that of the East, and that the culture of the Middle is again different from that of both East and West. Or if one tells them that in the West the great goals of mankind are sought, when they are sought, through the use of mediums who are put into a trance and are thereby consciously brought into a sub-earthly relationship to the spiritual worlds, out of which they speak of great historical aims. We could tell this repeatedly to Europeans yet they will not believe that in English-American countries there really exist societies in which the attempt is made to find out through questions cleverly put to mediums what the great goals of mankind are. People likewise do not believe that the Oriental obtains knowledge about the destiny of mankind not through mediums but on the mystical path. In the beautiful speeches of Rabindranath Tagore, easily available today, you can read what the Oriental thinks on a grand scale about the goals of mankind. These speeches are read as one reads the feature articles of any hack journalist; because today people distinguish little between a journalistic hack and persons of great spirituality like Rabindranath Tagore. They are not aware, I might say, that different racial substances can live side by side. What is valid for Middle Eruope I have put forward in public lectures for many years. It was not received as it should have been.

With this I only wish to point out that one may become aware of something that reaches beyond the egotistical fate of a man and is connected with the destiny of groups of men, so that we can make specific differentiations across the face of the earth. If one lifts his view toward comprehending human destiny in mankind as a whole, if one concerns himself intensely with what thus passes beyond personal destiny, then one tunes his soul to comprehending a higher reality than the Angel; actually that of the Archangel. Thoughts concerning the significance of an Archangel do not arise in one's soul if one remains in the regions concerned with egotistical man. Preachers may talk ever so much about the Divine; if they only preach within the confines of egotistical man they speak merely of the Angel. Calling it by a different name is just an untruth; it does not put the matter straight. Only if one begins to be interested in man's destiny as a unity over the whole earth does his soul begin to elevate itself to the Archangel.

Now let us pass on to something else. Let us feel what I have indicated in these lectures about the successive impulses of mankind's evolution. You will find that most of our leading citizens were educated in the classical schools —*Gymnasium*—during the years when the soul is pliable and flexible. These classical schools were not born out of the culture of our age but of the Greco-Latin age. If those Greeks and Romans had done what we did they would have established Egypto-Chaldean classical schools. They didn't do that; they took the subjects for their teaching from immediate life. We take them from the previous period and educate people accordingly. This is very significant, but we haven't recognized it. Had we done so a note would have sounded within the feminist movement that did not resound, and that is: Men, if their intelligence is to be specially trained, are sent into antiquated schools. There their brains become hardened. Women have the good fortune of not being admitted into the classical schools. We want to develop our intelligence in an original way; we want to show what can be developed in the present age if we are not made dull in our youth by Greco-Latin classical education.

These words did not resound, but in their place: Men have crept into and hidden under the Greco-Latin classical education, let us women do the same. Let us also become students of the classical schools.

So little has understanding spread for what is necessary! We must realize that in our present time we are not educated for our age but for the Greco-Latin culture. This is inserted into our lives. We must sense it. We must sense what, as Greco-Latin culture, acts in the leading people of today, in the so-called intellectuals. This is one aspect of what we carry within us in our spiritual education. We read no newspaper that does not contain Greco-Latin education; because, although writing in our national idiom, we actually write in the Greco-Latin form.

And in regard to our concept of rights we live in Romanism, again something antiquated. To be sure, the old national rights battle at times against Roman law, but they do not prevail. We must feel how a time that has passed lives in what man calls right and wrong in public life.

Only in economic life do we live in the present. This is a significant statement. Perhaps I may say in passing that many women use the concepts of the present in their cooking, in managing their households. In doing so they actually are the people of the present age; everything else that is carried into the present is antiquated. I do not present this matter of their cooking as something particularly desirable, but the other aspect is much less desirable, namely, that the souls of women also want to go back from the present to antiquated cultures. In looking upon our cultural surroundings we have not only what acts in space but also the effects of bygone eras. If we acquire a feeling for this, not only the past affects us but the future as well. *It is our task to let the future work into us.* Because, if there did not live in every person, however slightly aware of it, a kind of rebellion against the Hellenism of education and the Romanism of rights, if the future were not to ray in upon us, we would be pathetic creatures, really very pathetic creatures.

Besides space we must also consider time in our culture; that is to say, what as history reaches over into our present from the past and from the future. We, as people of the present, must realize that past and future play into our souls. Just as America, England, Asia, China, India—the East and the West as two opposites—have their effect upon us as Europeans, so do we carry Greece, Rome, and the future in us. If we are willing to focus our attention on the future by becoming aware of how what is past and what is coming into being live in our souls, then another attitude arises in us concerning human destiny, an attitude that transcends egotism and is different from what is aroused by a merely spatial consideration. Only if we develop this soul attitude is it possible for us to form concepts about the sphere of the Time Spirits, the Archai. That is to say, we come to the third rank of divine beings in the order of the Hierarchies.

It is good if man by such means places before himself these three Hierarchies in concepts and ideas, because the Spirits of Form who come next are much harder to comprehend. But it suffices for modern man if he attempts to penetrate beyond egotism into the sphere of the unegotistic, doing this repeatedly, and occupying himself with what I have just explained. I must emphasize again, that especially the training of teachers should make use of these facts. A teacher should not be permitted to instruct and educate without having acquired an idea of the egotism that strives toward the closest God, the Angel; without also having acquired a concept of the unegotistic, destiny-determining powers who are side by side in space above the earth, the Archangel beings; and without having acquired a concept of how past and future reach over into our culture, the Roman life of rights, the Greek spiritual substance, and the undefined rebel of the future, which saves us.

Mankind at present has little inclination to enter into these matters. Some time ago I repeatedly emphasized that it is one of our social tasks to derive from the present our educational subjects to be used during the time spent today in classical schools. To do as the Greeks themselves did, namely, take the subjects for education from present-day life.

Shortly after the time, and in the same place where I had spoken about the social importance of this problem (I do not wish to imply a causal connection but the matter has symptomatic meaning) there appeared in all the newspapers in that place a number of advertisements propagandizing the modern classical schools. I had delivered lectures characterizing classical education in the way I have done here. The advertisements declared what the German nation owes to the classical education of its youth, for "strengthening the national consciousness," "the national power," and so on. This was a few weeks before the Treaty of Versailles. These advertisements were signed by a variety of local figures from the schools and the department of education. What has to be brought out today as to the factual basis of mankind's evolution, is rejected. People let it bounce off; it does not touch the depths of the soul. For this reason it is so difficult to be active in the social sphere. One will never be able to take hold of the social question with the superficialities employed today. It is a deeply significant question that cannot be grasped if one will not look deeply into the nature of man and the world. Because this is so it should be evident how important are certain proposals offered by the threefold social order.

We must acquire an organ for what is necessary for our age, and it is difficult to acquire this organ in the spiritual sphere. For an education that has gradually been taken over by the State has deprived man of active striving; it has made him into a devoted member of the State structure. How do the majority of people live? Up to the sixth year of age man may live unhindered because the State does not yet consider him sanitary enough. The State would not like to devote itself to the tasks that have to be carried out in the first childhood years. Man is still left to the powers outside the State.

But then it lays claim to him and he is trained to fit the pattern of the State; he ceases to be a person and bears the stamp of the State. He strives to fit this pattern because it is instilled in him. He not only gets his keep from the State while he works but beyond the working age up to his death, in the form of a pension. It is the ideal of many people today to have a position that entitles them to a pension. The soul too becomes entitled to a pension, even beyond death, without any effort on its part, because it receives eternal bliss through the activity of the church. The church sees to that. Now it is very uncomfortable to hear that salvation lies in free spiritual striving which must be independent of the State. The State must only serve civil rights, where there will be no claim to a pension. This is reason enough for many to reject it, as we have occasion to notice again and again.

Concerning the most intimate spiritual life, the religious life, the world of the future will demand of man that he work for his immortality; that he let his soul be active so that it may receive into itself, through activity, the Divine, the Christ-impulse.

In the course of my life I have received many letters from church people who state that anthroposophy is fundamentally a fine thing, but it contradicts the simple Christian faith; that Christ has redeemed the soul, that one can attain salvation in Christ without any effort on one's part. People cannot let go of the "simple belief in the attainment of salvation through Christ." They believe themselves to be specially pious if they say or write something like that. But they are egotistical, extremely egotistical. They want to be passive in their souls and let it be the concern of the Divine to transport the soul, nicely pensioned, through the portal of death.

Matters are not so easy in that world conception in which, in future, the religious element must be created. Here one must understand that the presence of the Divine in the soul must be worked for. One will no longer be able just to surrender passively to the churches, which promise to carry the souls into the beyond. (The involvement of money for such service, a scandal in the past, has now fallen into disuse, but secretly it still plays a role in this process, also in obtaining special blessings.) But the transition to inner activity is what is needed for mankind, something it doesn't yet cherish very much.

In order to gain a feeling for what is necessary in this regard we must keep in mind, first, the metamorphosis of humanity since the time of ancient Egypt when the body was more of a plant-like nature. Should there be a relapse into that state in the present age, man would become sick and develop tumors and such things. Secondly, the fact that we carry our body as a corpse which can think, can understand. In this way we gain a feeling for what mankind needs, which is, to advance in the solving of social problems in the way this has to be done in the present time. We must no longer allow ourselves to consider such a matter as the social question as being utterly simple.

You see, this is what is so difficult at present: That people would like to be enlightened on the most important aspects of life by a few abstract statements. If a book like *The Threefold Social Order* contains more than a few abstract statements, if it contains the results of an observation of life, then people say they do not understand it. They consider it confusing. But this is the misfortune at present, that people do not wish to enter into what precisely they ought to enter into. For abstract sentences, completely lucid, refer to what is dead; the social element, however, ought to be alive. Here we must employ flexible ideas, flexible sentences, flexible forms. Therefore it is necessary that we not only reflect upon the transformation of single institutions, but that we really adjust ourselves to a genuine transformation in our thinking and learning, down to their innermost structure.

This is what I would like to leave with you today when I have to leave again for a few weeks. We must feel ourselves influenced by the working together of our anthroposophical and our social movement. I should like you to comprehend more and more why it is that the anthroposophically oriented science of the spirit must flow into the souls of men if anything is to be achieved in the social field. And I would bring close to your hearts what I have said repeatedly in various ways: It is of utmost importance to acknowledge that what we can acquire of anthroposophical knowledge is the true guide-line now for all action and striving; that we must have the courage to will to prevail with anthroposophy. The worst thing is that people in these days have so little courage for willing to prevail with what is needed. They permit their best will-forces to break down; though it is so necessary they do not will to carry through.

Learn to represent anthroposophy with courage. Receive graciously the people who show an interest in looking at this building which represents our spiritual striving. Rejoice in every single individual who shows even a little understanding. Meet with him. But do not take it to heart if your efforts are fruitless, and people meet our activities with evil intention, or, what is more frequent, with lack of understanding. Just resist it suitably. It is courage that is needed to bring our efforts through to good results. Let us think of ourselves as the handful of people whose destiny it is to know and to communicate to the world what it so sorely needs today. Let the people ridicule us and say that it is presumption to believe all this. It is true nevertheless. Saying to oneself, "It is true nevertheless,"—saying it so earnestly that it fills one's whole soul, this needs the inner courage we must have. May it permeate us as anthroposophical substance. Then we shall do what we have to do, every one at the place where he is. This I wanted to say to you today.

We are longing for the day when our activity through this building brings us closer to the outside world; our activity which in any case is very difficult. This building is the only one that takes into account the great destinies of mankind even in its forms, and it is very gratifying to see that attention is being paid to it. Something else, however, is necessary for favorable progress in social problems, and that is, that this building through its very forms, which are stronger than other modern architectural forms, should aid in the strengthening of humanity's spiritual powers; making men more amenable to what one wishes them to know, so that they may rise not only to the nature of the Angel, but to the Archangel, and to the Spirit of the Time.

With these words I take leave of you for a few weeks. I hope to be able then to continue these considerations, and that during this time we shall come into an intensive activity for our building itself. Because, my dear friends, we are justified in emphasizing on every hand that readiness for work, that joy in work is needed for all men. This will not come if people are not moved by great purposes. I believe that if people can be convinced that through the three-folding of the social organism they can attain an existence worthy of man, they will begin to work again. Otherwise they will continue to strike. For in the field of physical labor people need an impulse that takes hold of them in their inmost souls.

But we must show that our work has been fruitful in attaining at least one objective, and this radiates into the world. Only then can we give the impulse to mankind to overcome spiritually what is dead in our time. Let us think this over, my dear friends, until the time when we are together again and can speak further about these questions.